ANSWERS TO YOUR BIBLE VERSION QUESTIONS

DAVID W. DANIELS

CHICK
PUBLICATIONS
Ontario, Calif. 91761

For a complete list of distributors near you,
call us at (909) 987-0771, or visit us online at:
www.chick.com

Copyright © 2003 David W. Daniels

Published by:
CHICK PUBLICATIONS
P. O. Box 3500, Ontario, Calif. 91761-1019 USA
Tel: (909) 987-0771
Fax: (909) 941-8128
Web: www.chick.com
Email: postmaster@chick.com

Printed in the United States of America

ISBN: 0-7589-0507-6

This pastor thought he was building faith, but actually he was tearing it down. How much error does the Bible have? 5%? 10%? If it contains only a "few errors" how can I know which part is the truth and which is not? And which Bible is the most correct? The faith of Christians is being undermined by pastors who do not believe what God said:

> The words of the LORD are pure words: as silver tried in a furnace of earth, purified seven times. Thou shalt keep them, O LORD, <u>thou shalt preserve them</u> from this generation for ever. (Psalm 12:6-7)

A Bible with a "few" errors is simply not good enough. If God kept His promise, we should be able to determine exactly what ARE God's words, and then place them in people's hands. We must get the answers to some important questions:

- Where did the Bible come from?
- Did the Roman Catholic religion give us the Bible, as they claim?
- Is the Bible translated correctly?
- Is the King James Bible error-free?
- What's wrong with other versions?

This book answers these and other questions. As you read them and their answers you will find the proof you need. You will know for a certainty why the King James Bible is God's perfectly preserved words in English, a Bible you can trust with your eternal destiny.

Contents

CHAPTER 1

Where Did The Bible Come From?

CHAPTER 2

Is The True Bible Roman Catholic?

CHAPTER 3

Is The King James Bible Translated Correctly?

CHAPTER 4

Is The KJV Text Error-Free?

CHAPTER 5

What's Wrong With The Other Versions?

Missing Words

Different Words

Corrupt Manuscripts

Other Languages

CHAPTER 6

What's Wrong With KJV Look-Alikes?

CHAPTER 7

What Will I Do?

Chapter 1

Where Did The Bible Come From?

QUESTION

How did God preserve His words to this day?

ANSWER

God preserved copies of His words down through time, using four main languages He chose for that purpose. All through history, God made several choices as to the languages in which He would communicate His message.

Choice 1: Hebrew

From at least as far back as Abraham (around 2000 BC) to the destruction of the second Temple in Jerusalem in 70 AD, God chose the Semitic languages, especially Hebrew, to communicate to His chosen people. God gave His law in Hebrew to teach men that they were sinners, and in need of a Saviour.

Choice 2: Greek

In the first century AD, God made a second choice. The main language of the world for three centuries had been Greek. God used that language to give the New Testament for the world to read. And it spread like wildfire.

The devil recognized the huge potential of God's Word in a "world" language, so he moved quickly to counter it. He prepared a fake "Bible" in Alexandria, Egypt. The Old Testament portion is called the "Septuagint" and the New Testament portion is called the "Alexandrian text." This corruption was a "Greek" Bible, but with the poison of the Apocrypha mixed in, made to look like real scripture. The Alexandrian "Bible" also perverted the New Testament[1], taking out many of God's words and substituting man's ideas. This laid the groundwork for Satan's plan to spread religious lies, and subvert the true faith.

Choice 3: Old Latin

From about 120 AD until the 1500s, God used a third language to communicate His truths, in addition to Hebrew and Greek. While the first copies of the New Testament in Greek were being made and passed around, God directed other Christians to translate His preserved words into Old Latin. This language was being spoken more and more in Europe, and became an "international" language as Greek had been. The Old Latin Bible was known as the "Vulgate," which means "common Bible." Once again, God's words were spreading, and many Europeans began translating these Old Latin scriptures into their own languages.

The devil responded by preparing a counterfeit "Vulgate" in Rome. By the 300s, the Roman religion claimed to be true Christianity, and a new "Bible" was made from the perverted Alexandrian writings. It included the Apocryphal books that the early church had rejected. But to make it convincing, they also put in *some* scriptures that were like the preserved Old Latin Bible as well. There were now two Latin "Vulgates," dramatically different from one another. The true Christians knew the difference between the true and the false "Vulgates."

The devil knew what he had to do next. He had to destroy the true Latin Vulgate, and the people who held it so dearly. The Roman Catholic armies hunted down and martyred those who were caught possessing the true Latin Vulgate. But they were never able to completely replace the true Latin Vulgate with the corrupted Roman Catholic Latin Vulgate. God was preserving His words.

Choice 4: English

Around 700-800 AD, English, a new "world" language began to develop. God began laying the groundwork to use this language to trigger a massive missionary movement. In the 1500s William Tyndale worked to translate the Bible from the accurate Greek and Hebrew manuscripts that God had so carefully preserved. English-speaking people after him continued the effort to translate and perfect a Bible that matched the ancient scriptures. One of the best of these is the Geneva Bible.

English was a language in the midst of change. But by 1604 God used King James I[2] of England to commission a group of learned men[3] to accumulate scriptures in Hebrew, Greek, Latin and English as well as other languages. Their assignment was to translate[4] God's words into the most accurate English possible. In early 1611 they published the Authorized Version, also known as the King James Bible. From the day it was published, the King James Bible circulated around the world, and missionaries translated Bibles from this precious book.

The devil pulled out all the stops on this one. By the 1800s he had inspired a whole movement to discredit and destroy the King James Bible. Today, we have a multitude of translations that change, remove and add to God's preserved words. But God has always kept the true scriptures in the hands of his people.

In making the four choices of language as described above, God was not trying to indicate that any single language was more expressive or better than another. Rather, He chose these languages because they suited His purpose at a particular time in history to carry out His plan. The choices were God's. Outside of Israel, Hebrew was never a universal language. Ancient Greek is no longer a universal language, nor is Latin. But by guiding the production of a perfect Bible in English, God kept His promise. For our time, in a language read around the world, God preserved His words.

Footnotes

[1]See page 131, "Is the Lord's Prayer in Your Bible?"

[2]See page 19, "Why is the King James Bible called the "Authorized Version"? How was it authorized?"

[3]See page 21, "Who were the translators of the King James Bible?"

[4]See page 28, "What method was used to translate the King James Bible?"

QUESTION

How do I show which Bible is correct to those who refuse to hear "King James only" arguments?

ANSWER

The key is to show them how the broad evidence of history tells us which Greek text is correct. It then becomes easy to know which Bible we can trust. First, please remember the simple fact that there are two streams of Bible history. The first line comes straight from the Apostles and people of Antioch. To date, 5,322 manuscripts, and the broad evidence of history support that line.

The Broad Evidence of History

This evidence for this stream spans from some of our oldest manuscripts to some of the least ancient. These manuscripts are in agreement with those of the persecuted believers, such as the Vaudois in the French Alps. They received the Scriptures from apostolic groups from Antioch of Syria about AD 120 and finished their translation by AD 157, according to Calvin's successor, Theodore Beza. These manuscripts influenced one of the greatest events in Christian history: the Protestant Reformation.

The Polluted Stream

The other stream comes from questionable sources. About the time of Christ, a Jewish man named Philo decided to blend pagan Greek philosophy with Judaism. The so-called "Christians" who came after him in Alexandria were not much better. Though they talked about "Jesus" and "Christianity," they did not believe that Jesus was God. They also did not believe that the Old

Testament detailed literal events. It was a school in this pagan city that decided to write their own copies of the Bible.

The problem is that they changed the Scriptures, while saying they were copying them. They used the heretic Marcion's Lord's Prayer in Luke, for example. (See Question 43, "Is the Lord's Prayer in Your Bible?"). From there it goes downhill.

In truth there are only a handful of semi-complete "Bibles" from Alexandria, Egypt. The only other texts from there are literally pieces of paper. The grand total of manuscripts is only 44. Of those 44, only 3 are taken very seriously: the Sinaiticus (Aleph), the Alexandrinus (A) and Vaticanus (B).

But there is a very big problem. It is rare that these three ever agree. Between Sinaiticus and Vaticanus, for example, it is extremely difficult to find just two successive verses that agree.

Look at the Lord's Prayer in Luke again. Between codices Aleph, A [Alexandrinus], B [Vaticanus], C [Ephraemi Rescriptus] and D [Bezae Cantabrigiensis] there is no agreement in 32 out of 45 words. That means these major books only agree in 13 out of 45 words!

A Visual Image

Here's one way to explain the difference between the manuscripts. Imagine a stadium with 5,366 people. 5,322 of them are in harmony, agreeing with one another and enjoying themselves. But there are also 44 other people. These are not like the first. They dislike the crowd around them and slander their words when they can. But they have another problem: they also disagree with each other.

Which group would you rather listen to? The one with people in one accord, or the one that is filled with discord? The one that knows what it is saying, or the one that cannot agree on what it wants to say? The answer is obvious.

Where Do the Two Streams Lead?

A tree is known by its fruit. Where, then, do these two streams of Bibles lead?

The Alexandrian manuscripts fell into disuse, and many were relegated to a desert trashcan. A number of "scholars" tried to make the expensive codices better by changing the words to be more like the other stream, but they finally gave up. Those are the many corrections we see in the Sinaiticus and Vaticanus.

But where do the Alexandrian manuscripts lead? Straight to the Roman Catholic institution. They were used by Constantine with the help of Eusebius. They became the basis of the Apocrypha and many incorrect readings in the Roman Catholic Bible. They were used to dominate and subject true believers under a false religion. This was the Bible of the persecutors.

Alexandrian Bibles are legion. Such are the NIV, NASV, ASV, RV, TEV, GNB, Living, NCV, RSV, NRSV, etc., but also Catholic Bibles as the New American Bible, the Jerusalem and New Jerusalem Bibles.

The Antiochian manuscripts (from which we got the King James Bible) continued to be used and were passed down by faithful Christians from generation to generation. The Vaudois, for example, passed them down faithfully by even having their children memorize whole books of the Bible. These faithful people hand-copied little Bibles they could fit in their heavy garments. They were ready to give an answer, literally "in season and out of season"!

And where do the Antiochian manuscripts lead? Straight to the Protestant Reformation. Wesley and writers of the Geneva Bible actually saw the Vaudois as a "pre-Reformation" group, even as the "two witnesses" who were protected by God in Revelation. (See pp. 115-116). That is how much they were indebted to these faithful.

Antiochian Bibles are easily recognizable. They are the Bibles of the Reformation: the Reina-Valera (Spanish), Diodati (Italian), and all the other Protestant Bibles published between the 1530s and 1600s. In English they are the Tyndale, Coverdale, Matthew's, Great Bible, Bishops Bible, Geneva and King James.

The fruit, for example, of the King James Bible in English is easily discernible. Look at many English-speaking Protestant denominations that were formed in an effort to get "back to the Bible." The King James Bible was the starting point. The pilgrim Puritans in the USA switched from the Geneva to the King James in their next generation, despite the fact that they had used the Geneva since the 1560s. And ironically, the churches and Christians called "extreme Fundamentalists" and "right-wing extremists" are simply the churches that did not leave the fundamentals.

There are two kinds of churches: those that left their founding doctrines and those that stuck to them. There are also two kinds of Bibles: those that follow corrupt and perverted Alexandrian texts and/or Roman Catholic doctrine, and those that follow the line of preservation through godly and persecuted Christian brethren.

The choice is obvious.

QUESTION

Why is the King James Bible called the "Authorized Version"? How was it authorized?

ANSWER

Despite stories to the contrary, King James, in no uncertain terms, clearly authorized the translation of the Bible that now bears his name.

[Note: This is a drastically shortened account of the birth of God's preserved words in English. Longer accounts are available, as in Final Authority: A Christian's Guide to the King James Bible, by William P. Grady, available from Chick Publications.]

Sanctioning the Authorized Version

When Elizabeth I died on April 1, 1603, she had seen 130 editions of the New Testament and the Bible published during her 45 years as Queen of England. James VI of Scotland, son of Mary, "Queen of Scots," became James I of England.

Four days later, on his way to London, a delegation of Puritan ministers met James, asking him to hear their grievances against the Church of England. James consented, and on January of 1604, four Puritans came to express their troubles at Hampton Court, in front of King James and over 50 Anglican (Church of England) officials. One by one each request was rejected, until the Puritan group's leader, John Rainolds said these famous words:

> "May your Majesty be pleased to direct that the Bible be now translated, [since] such versions as are extant [are] not answering to the original."

At first, Bishop Bancroft of London was dead-set against it, saying, "If every man's humor might be followed, there would be no end to translating." But the King made it clear he liked the idea. Not too long later Bancroft wrote this to a friend:

> I move you in his majesty's name that... no time may be overstepped by you for the better furtherance of this holy work... You will scarcely conceive how earnest his majesty is to have this work begun!

When this Bible was translated, the title page was printed basically as you find it today in Cambridge Bibles:

THE
HOLY BIBLE
CONTAINING THE
OLD AND NEW TESTAMENTS

TRANSLATED OUT OF THE ORIGINAL TONGUES:
AND WITH THE FORMER TRANSLATIONS
DILIGENTLY COMPARED AND REVISED
BY HIS MAJESTY'S SPECIAL COMMAND

APPOINTED TO BE READ IN CHURCHES

The King James Bible was "Authorized" to be translated as God's Word for the English-speaking people of the world.

QUESTION

Who were the translators of the King James Bible?

ANSWER

God brought together over 54 of the finest Bible translators English has ever known, to translate the King James Bible.

Researching the Translators

For twenty years (the 1830s to the 1850s) researcher Alexander McClure pored over records to learn all he could about who translated the King James Bible. His resulting book, *Translators Revived: A Biographical Memoir of the Authors of the English Version of the Holy Bible*[1], stands as a monument to these dedicated Christian men. I highly recommend it.

A Few Short Examples

Here are some of the qualified translators of the King James Bible.

John Harman, M.A., New College, Oxford

In 1585 he had been appointed King's Professor of Greek. He had published Latin translations of Calvin's and Beza's sermons, and was also adept in Greek. He was a member of the New Testament group that met at Oxford.

John Spencer

At 19 years of age he had been elected Greek lecturer for Corpus Christi College in Oxford University. It was written of him, "Of his eminent scholarship there can be no question." He was a member of the New Testament group (Romans through Jude) that met at Westminster.

Thomas Bilson

McClure wrote that he was "so complete in divinity, so well skilled in languages, so read in the Fathers and Schoolmen, so judicious in making use of his readings, that at length he was found to be no longer a soldier, but commander in chief in the spiritual warfare" (*Translators Revived*, pp. 214-416).

Dr. George Abbot, B.D., D.D.

Dr. Abbot started at Oxford in 1578, getting his B.D. in 1593 and at 35 years of age both received his doctorate and became first Master of University College, and later Vice Chancellor. He became Bishop of Lichfield in 1609 and Archbishop of Canterbury in 1611. He was regarded as "the head of the Puritans within the Church of England." He was in the Oxford New Testament group.

Sir Henry Saville

In 1565 Sir Saville was Fellow of Merton College and Warden in 1585. By 1596 he was Provost of Eton College and tutor to Queen Elizabeth I. He founded the Savillian professorships of Mathematics and Astronomy at Oxford. His many works include an 8-volume set of the writings of Chrysostom[2]. He also worked in the New Testament group at Oxford.

Lancelot Andrewes

From Terence H. Brown, (Secretary of the Trinitarian Bible Society, London, England) comes this description of Westminster committee member Lancelot Andrewes:

He "... had his early education at Coopers Free School and Merchant Taylors School, where his rapid progress in the study of the ancient languages was brought to the notice of Dr. Watts, the founder of some scholarships at Pembroke Hall, Cambridge. Andrewes was sent to that College, where he took his B.A. degree and soon afterward was elected Fellow. He then took his Master's degree and began to study divinity and achieved great distinction as a lecturer. He was raised to several positions of influence in the Church of England and distinguished himself as a diligent and excellent preacher, and became Chaplain to Queen Elizabeth I. King James I promoted him to be Bishop of Chester in 1605 and also gave him the influential position of Lord Almoner. He later became Bishop of Ely and Privy Counsellor. Toward the end of his life he was made Bishop of Winchester.

"It is recorded that Andrewes was a man of deep piety and that King James had such great respect for him that in his presence he refrained from the levity in which he indulged at other times. A sermon preached at Andrewes' funeral in 1626 paid tribute to his great scholarship:

'His knowledge in Latin, Greek, Hebrew, Chaldee, Syriac and Arabic, besides fifteen modern languages was so advanced that he may be ranked as one of the rarest linguists in Christendom. A great part of five hours every day he spent in prayer, and in his last illness he spent all his time in prayer — and when both voice and eyes and hands failed in their office, his countenance showed that he still prayed and praised God in his heart, until it pleased God to receive his blessed soul to Himself.'"

Transcending Their Human Limits

Gustavus S. Paine, author of *The Men Behind the King James Version,* made this assessment about the work of the combined translators:

> "Though we may challenge the idea of word-by-word inspiration, we surely must conclude that these were men able, in their profound moods, to transcend their human limits. In their own words, *they spake as no other men spake because they were filled with the Holy Ghost.* Or, in the clumsier language of our time, they so adjusted themselves to each other and to the work as to achieve a unique coordination and balance, functioning thereafter as an organic entity—no mere mechanism equal to the sum of its parts, but *a whole greater than all of them.*[3]

While these scholars were perfectly suited for the task of translation individually, they still had to agree on every single word of the Bible. That meant man's mere opinion could not be allowed to stand in the text.

The One Who Started It All

But these translators were standing on the shoulders of great men and Christians who went before them. And one man did more for the English Bible than any single person before or since: William Tyndale. He was ordained a priest around his late teens, in 1502. By 1515 he had earned his M.A. at Oxford and later transferred to Cambridge. It was there that he came upon the preserved Greek New Testament of Erasmus, and at the same time as Martin Luther, he came to understand the truth of the gospel. Tyndale began preaching and teaching the gospel message, which made the Roman Catholics angry with him, branding him a heretic. One day, while proving a "learned" Roman Catholic scholar wrong, the papist cried out, "It were better for us to be without **God's laws,** than without the Pope's!" To which Tyndale prophetically replied,

> **"I defy the Pope, and all his laws; and if God spare my life, ere many years, I will cause a boy that driveth the plough to know more of the Scripture than *thou* dost!"**

This changed Tyndale forever. He wrote about this incident,

> "Which thing only moved me to translate the New Testament. Because I had perceived by experience, how that it was impossible to establish the lay people in any truth, except the Scriptures were plainly laid before their eyes in the mother tongue" (*Translators Revived*, p. 23).

Tyndale was well suited to his task. Spalatin, a friend of Martin Luther, wrote this in his diary of what professor Herman Buschius told him about Tyndale and his New Testament:

> "The work was translated by an Englishman staying there with two others,—a man so skilled in the seven languages, Hebrew, Greek, Latin, Italian, Spanish, English, and French, that which-ever he spake, you would suppose it his native tongue" (*Translators Revived*, pp. 27-28)

By the time Tyndale was betrayed by his friend, imprisoned and nearly frozen during a cold winter in his cell, he had translated the New Testament into English, along with some Old Testament books, and had trained at least two others to carry on his work. But he wasn't finished. Even when burnt at the stake on October 6, 1536, he cried out prophetically:

"Lord! Open the King of England's eyes"4

That very day a copy of Tyndale's New Testament was being printed by the King's own printer!

Conclusion

Tyndale's work of translation was so excellent that easily 70% of the words of the Bible are Tyndale's. God had set the standard.

Over the next century, God's preserved words were translated and revised by many scholars, a great many "good translations." These, along with God's preserved words in Italian, Spanish, French, Dutch and other languages were all "good translations." But the goal of the king's translators of 1604-1611 was not to write a new Bible from scratch, nor was it to make a translation from the Roman Catholic perversions:

> "Truly, good Christian Reader, we never thought from the beginning that we should need to make a new translation, nor yet to make of a bad one a good one; ... but to make a good one better, or out of many good ones one principal good one, not justly to be excepted against; that hath been our endeavor, that our mark" (The Translators to the Reader, 1611 KJV, ninth page).

And that is exactly what God did. Throughout history God preserved His words. And culminating with over 54 dedicated, learned Christian men, God put His words in English in its perfection in one final translation: The King James Bible.

Footnotes

[1]It may be read online at http://www.wilderness-cry.net/bible_study/translators/.

[2]Chrysostom was a 4th century Greek-speaking minister and writer.

[3]Gustavus Paine, *The Men Behind the King James Version*, p. 173, quoted in *Crowned With Glory: The Bible from Ancient Text to Authorized Version* by Thomas Holland, p. 90 (Emphasis mine).

[4]Dr. William Grady, *Final Authority*, p. 137.

QUESTION
What method was used to translate the King James Bible?

ANSWER

King James had no part whatsoever in the translation of the Bible that now bears his name. But there were 47-54 scholars, however, whom God used to bring us His preserved words in English.

Translating the Authorized Version

54 scholars were appointed in 1604, and a few overseers were also present, who went from group to group. In time, through death, the number of translators diminished to 47. They were given three locations to work: Oxford, Cambridge and Westminster. And two groups worked at each location, making a total of six groups. The Bible was also divided up into six sections. Each group took one section, working on one book at a time.

First, each translator made his own translation of the book, which was reviewed by each other member of the group. Then the whole group reviewed the book. When they all agreed on the translation, they sent it to the other five groups for evaluation. Those groups then returned it to the original committee, marking anything they disagreed with. The original group would then go over the book again.

When all six committees finished with the book, it was sent, with any differences that were left, to a special committee made up of one leader from each of the six groups. They solved any remaining problems, and the book was sent to the printers.

But they did not work in secret, as did the "Revisers" in 1871-1881. At any time, the translators could ask an outside scholar for his understanding, and anyone could find out about the progress. The churches were kept informed at all times.

In all, every single verse of the Bible was carefully examined and decided upon a total of fourteen times, by as many as 50 or more people! This made it impossible for any one translator to impose his personal viewpoint on a passage. He had to have logical reasons for a translation that were good enough to persuade every other scholar before it could be written into the text. There was no "private interpretation" here! (2 Peter 1:20-21)

God superintended the translation, so that what we need to know from the Bible has been accurately translated for us. We do have, translated in English for the world, God's perfectly preserved words.

QUESTION

Wasn't the King James Bible translated from only half a dozen manuscripts, none of which were earlier than the 10th century (900s) AD?

ANSWER

This is true, but it misses an important point. It is true that the manuscripts used were copies of copies of copies written over many centuries. These "new" manuscripts match up with over 5,000 others, some just as old as those from Alexandria, Egypt. Over 99% of the manuscripts we have found, ancient and modern, show an amazing agreement with each other. This is a testimony to God's preservation of His words!

Contrast this to the Alexandrian writings, used by the Roman Catholic religion and almost all "modern scholars." The only 44 manuscripts called "Alexandrian," many copied in the same school, not only do not agree with the vast majority, but they do not match up with each other!

But God's preserved words, descended from the apostles and sent from Antioch (Acts 11:26), were so important to the true Christians that they continued to be accurately copied century after century!

How important could the Alexandrian writings be, if these "scholars" could not even get together one clear Bible?

God preserved His words. The King James Bible is the accurate and complete translation of them, from Greek in Antioch of Syria into the English language.

QUESTION

Is there an edition of the *Textus Receptus* in Greek and Hebrew that you can recommend for those studying the languages as they are used in the Bible?

ANSWER

I have a very simple suggestion. Grab an interlinear King James New Testament (or Old Testament or single-volume Greek/Hebrew Bible) and correct it anywhere the translation disagrees with the King James. I am not kidding.

Let me give you an example.

The Interlinear New Testament by George Ricker Berry is a fine text to start with. It has a 99% accurate Greek text[1], and the King James on the side column. When you read Acts 3 and 4 you will notice that the King James says, "his Son Jesus," the Berry interlinear says "servant." Just read "Son" instead of "servant" and you will do fine. The only Hebrew Old Testament I know that uses the text in the King James is the one by Jay Green. The Hebrew is very very small, and sometimes hard to read. But it is the correct Hebrew text. When Green wrongly disagrees with the King James word, just substitute the right one and you will do well.

Why do we need to go to all this trouble? Because the translators of the Interlinear sometimes thought they knew more than God's blessed Bible translators of the King James Bible. Sometimes their teachers taught them the King James word was wrong, and they made up their own word to switch for the accurate King James word. However they did it, modern interlinear writers again created a different Bible from the King James! But the KJV is so accurate to the Greek and Hebrew that if one understands the English translation of the original language, he will also understand the correct meanings of Greek and Hebrew words.

Footnotes
[1]Why are our modern Greek texts of the New Testament, even of the *Textus Receptus*, different from the King James? In the late 1800s, when a man named Scrivener worked to re-create the Greek text of the King James Bible, he made a very close but slightly different Greek text. He did not have all the manuscripts the King James translators had, so he used only the texts in his possession! That made his *Textus Receptus* different from the accurate King James text. I sincerely hope someone will make a perfect Greek New Testament, to match our perfect English New Testament, the KJV.

QUESTION
Why should I read the King James translation and not just the Greek and Hebrew?

ANSWER
It is important that people in each generation learn and read the Greek and Hebrew manuscripts, but there is also a danger some may face in this.

Why Learn Greek and Hebrew?
As questions arise, each generation of believers needs to have Greek and Hebrew scholars that can look at the broad evidence of history. God uses history to testify that He kept His promise: God has indeed preserved His words.

The Danger
The problem is that many people think that a year or two of Greek or Hebrew qualifies them to translate their own Bibles. But they forget that in numerous languages, there are many words that can have one or more meanings, depending on the context. What they really do, though, is take a dictionary or lexicon and pick whatever meaning they feel is right. But those who translated the King James Bible knew the Greek and Hebrew, like you or I might know the English language.

The following actually happened. Shortly after the King James was translated, one of the translators, Dr. Richard Kilbye, an expert in Hebrew and Greek, visited a church with his friend, Bishop Sanderson. In that church, a young preacher spent a great deal of time criticizing words in the KJV and telling what he thought the Bible **should** say. He used up most of his time on one particular word.

That evening the young preacher was invited to dinner, along with Dr. Kilbye. Dr. Kilbye then told how they had looked at the **three** reasons given by the preacher, but then found **thirteen** better reasons to translate the word as it is.

This preacher (with more humility than most modern critics) admitted his error to the learned doctor and stopped preaching at that church.

The King James Bible was translated by people who **were** experts in the Hebrew and Greek. They reviewed every verse of the Bible **fourteen times**, and had to come to agreement on every word they used. This guaranteed that the Bible didn't just have some person's opinion in the text, like many modern perversions.

The King James Bible is God's expression in the English language, of His preserved words. He preserved them from the creation of the world to the present day. All of my Greek and Hebrew studies to this day have shown me that I can trust what God preserved in the King James Bible.

QUESTION

Are the "Bible Codes" a miraculous witness to the Bible? Several claim that the Bible Code points to the Son of God as Yeshua. But what does the Word of God say? In Nehemiah 8:17 according to the original Hebrew Text and the Old King James Version of 1611, it is made certain that Yeshua (Jeshua), is the son of Nun. Obviously, the son of Nun can never be the son of God. Therefore, isn't the Bible Code fake, and couldn't it be used for total blasphemy?

ANSWER

You're right. There is no way to tell whether the "Bible Codes" are being used to show divinity of the Lord Jesus Christ or of Joshua, Moses' successor. Obviously Joshua son of Nun was in no way the same as Jesus Christ, the Son of the living God. And there is another problem. When using the program to find "Jesus," His name could also be spelled "Jeshua," "Jehoshua" or "Jahshua," in Hebrew. With the right settings, the so-called "Bible Code" can say whatever we want it to say.

For instance, I was able to use a Bible Code program to "find" the blasphemy that "John Lennon is a god." If I have nothing but consonants to search, I can probably find anything I'm looking for, somewhere in the Hebrew Old Testament.

I take no stock in "Bible codes." What God said plainly in His preserved words is much too clear to rely on supposed "patterns" in skipping from letter to letter. The most exciting "mystery" in the Bible is a revealed mystery, the Gospel (Ephesians 6:19).

What God wants us to understand He made obvious in the Scriptures.

Chapter 2

Is the True Bible Roman Catholic?

QUESTION
Didn't the Roman Catholic church give us the Bible?

ANSWER
No. The Catholic church tried to take credit for what the Lord did without their help. Here is a short history of the Bible.

Old Testament

The Old Testament was written by Moses, David and Solomon, prophets, seers and kings. There was no "church" of any kind to claim responsibility for it. God inspired individuals to bring God's word to the people. The Old Testament is the recorded revelation of God up until about 400 BC.

The Inter-Testamental Period

The time between about 400 BC and about 5 BC is usually called the Years of Prophetic Silence. This is because God created a process that lasted 400 years to create a world climate ready for the coming of the promised Messiah. There was no "church" at this time, either. But there was the new creation of the "synagogue," since the Jewish people needed to worship God and did not have the Temple when they were in exile. When many came back 400-500 BC, they already had functional synagogues; and even though the Temple was being rebuilt by those returning from exile, the synagogue idea remained and more were built. This was the beginning of the "congregation" or "church" as we have it today.

But there was no Scripture being written during this period. That was yet to come after one came "in the spirit and power of Elias" (Luke 1:17).

The Time of Christ

It is likely that Matthew (Levi) the tax collector and later disciple of Jesus took notes of what happened during Jesus' ministry. However, it is also true that were God in the flesh living among you, His words would burn into your soul. I am sure, as the apostles clearly recollected as they wrote the New Testament (2 Peter 1:16-21; 1 John 1:1-3; 4:14), they could not escape the image and words of Jesus Christ, God the Son and Son of God, when He spoke into their hearts (Luke 9:44; 24:32).

But it wasn't a "church" that made them write 2 Timothy 3:16-17:

> All scripture is given by inspiration of God, and is profitable for doctrine, for reproof, for correction, for instruction in righteousness: That the man of God may be perfect, throughly furnished unto all good works.

And 2 Peter 1:19-21:

> We have also a more sure word of prophecy; whereunto ye do well that ye take heed, as unto a light that shineth in a dark place, until the day dawn, and the day star arise in your hearts: Knowing this first, that no prophecy of the scripture is of any private interpretation. For the prophecy came not in old time by the will of

man: but holy men of God spake as they were
moved by the Holy Ghost.

God the Holy Spirit inspired them, perfectly and
accurately, to write the words of God for the church. The
church did not "inspire" anything.

The Church Age

When the apostles wrote their letters, the congregations
received them. They read them. They spread them. They
copied them for other brethren in Christ Jesus. And they
recognized their authority in the Christian's life. So the
Scriptures were produced by men of God, not by "the
church." But they were produced FOR the church.

The last book of the Bible was Revelation, written about
96 AD, just before the apostle John died around 100 AD.
After the apostles died, the churches continued to collect
the letters they did not have, to read them and understand
the authority under God by which they wrote.

But no one else shared that place. There is an "Epistle of
Barnabas" (which bears no proof it was written by
Barnabas), which many think was penned in the first
century. But the difference between its message of
salvation and of the apostolic writings is too easy to see. If
you believe the Scriptures, you cannot believe the so-
called "epistle of Barnabas."

There are the writings of Polycarp, disciple of John
(when John was very aged). There are writings of Clement
and others. But those are all writings of Christians. Just
Christians. Some were even martyrs, but their writings
depended on the Scriptures—they were not Scripture
themselves. Anyone who would base their faith on them
would have a horrid foundation, just as if there were

"Lutherans" today, learning of God's word only what they find in Martin Luther's writings. Interesting writing, at times fine "inspirational" writing. Inspired? Not a chance.

The Roman Catholic religion has had only one aim from its earliest, pagan and political origins: to destroy the true Christians, and to destroy their Bible. That is why they substituted the corrupt Alexandrian perversions of scripture, instead of using the preserved, prophetic and apostolic words of God as found in Antioch of Syria, where "the disciples were first called Christians" (Acts 11:26). That is why they also added the Alexandrian writings we now call "Apocrypha" to their perverted bibles. That is why they used their Jesuits to infiltrate the Protestant Seminaries, Colleges and Bible Schools. Their Jesuits became the "teachers" and planted seeds of doubt in the Christians' minds. These doubt-ridden Christians then taught at other colleges and schools. All the while they planted that same seed of doubt of God's word in their students.

The stage was set: once people no longer believed in God's preserved words, which we find perfectly presented in the King James Bible, they were ripe for destruction. Now, 120 years after the switch from God's Word to devil's lies (the King James abandoned for the Alexandrian texts), while pretending to "improve" our copies of God's words, they really set up the abandonment of God's words. Now almost every Bible in the English-speaking world (and most other languages) is just another re-translation of the Alexandrian polluted stream.

Another way to view it is that the Scriptures as we find them preserved in the King James is like God's fountain:

For my people have committed two evils; they

have forsaken me the fountain of living waters,
and hewed them out cisterns, broken cisterns,
that can hold no water. (Jeremiah 2:13)

That's the point. The bible spewed out by the Catholic
church, which now almost all Protestants and other
Christians use... *simply doesn't hold water.*

QUESTION

How did the Catholic church hide the Bible, since the first printed Bible (Gutenberg's) was Roman Catholic?

ANSWER

The Roman Catholic religion did hide the Bible from the common people. There were two ways in which this happened.

First, the Roman Catholic leaders by the Middle Ages usually did not know the Bible. Many people bought their position as priests. Many did not have a Bible at all; but more importantly, many local priests did not even know how to read.

Second, the Roman Catholic religion did not even use a genuine Bible. Their book was from the polluted Alexandrian stream. The real Bible was kept by many people the Roman Catholics persecuted and murdered.

Since the Roman Catholic religion did not want the true Bible in the hands of the people, they 1) used a false Bible, 2) persecuted people who did have a true Bible, and 3) did not let even the perverted Bible be published widely in the language of the people.

The Gutenberg Bible you refer to was a Roman Catholic Vulgate, not a preserved Bible. Although he invented the movable-type printing press, he did not do mass copies of even the perverted Bible. That did not occur until a couple of events happened.

First, the city in which Gutenberg worked was invaded in 1462, spreading the printing press invention to Rome, Paris, Krakow (Poland) and Westminster (England). Second, the Reformers got hold of preserved Bibles and used these presses to print thousands of Bibles and Christian literature for the people.

You are right that Bibles before this had to be copied by hand. But the incredible historical fact is this: That is exactly what those who had the preserved Bibles did. It was these many, handwritten copies of God's preserved words that so blessed, informed and converted the earliest Protestants of the Reformation. Just like you can find it in the King James Bible today.

QUESTION

Wasn't Erasmus, creator of the *Textus Receptus*, really a Roman Catholic?

ANSWER

Desiderius Erasmus was raised a Catholic, and did not openly "leave" the Roman Catholic religion, but he did not believe Roman Catholic doctrine either. In fact, his best friends and defenders were the Christians, like the Anabaptists and Martin Luther. Here is proof from researcher Gail Riplinger.

Gail Riplinger, author of *New Age Bible Versions* and *The Language of the King James Bible*[1] has written another excellent book, *In Awe of Thy Word (2003)*.[2] In chapter 27 she proves the Christian, Biblical beliefs of Erasmus and exposes the evil motives of the people who try to defame him. The following research can be found in her book.

Did Erasmus' contemporaries believe he was a Catholic?

The following are quotes from various researchers:

"In the midst of the group of Protestant scholars who had long been his truest friends, and so far as is known, without relations of any sort with the Roman Catholic Church, he died."[3]

"He died at Basel in 1536, committed to neither party, but amid an admiring circle of friends who were all on the Reformed side."[4]

[He was an] "ex monk ... a Protestant pastor preached his funeral sermon and the money that he left was used to help Protestant refugees."[5]

"In 1559 Pope Paul IV 'placed everything Erasmus had ever written' on The Index of Forbidden Books."[6]

"[H]e was branded an impious heretic, and his works were forbidden to Catholic readers"[7]

"The Council of Trent condemned Erasmus' translation"[8] of the Bible. It is clear that his Bible was not a perverted Roman Catholic Vulgate translation at all.

"In 1527, Spanish "monks of the Inquisition began a systematic scrutiny of Erasmus' works, with a view to having [Erasmus] condemned as a heretic."[9]

In His Own Words

Listen to Erasmus explain his own views:

"All I ask for is the leisure to live wholly to God, to repent of the sins of my foolish youth, to study Holy Scriptures, and to read or write something of real value. I could do nothing of this, in a convent."[10]

In 1505 he wrote,

"I shall sit down to Holy Scriptures with my whole heart, and devote the rest of my life to it... all these three years I have been working entirely at Greek and have not been playing with it."[11]

Here are some other quotes, cited by Riplinger:

"As to me, all I have sought has been to open my contemporaries' eyes and bring them back from ritual to true Christianity."

"Read the Gospels... and see how we have degenerated."

"A man of piety would feel that he could not employ his time better than in bringing little ones to Christ."

"We must forget ourselves, and think first of Christ's glory."[12]

Are these the words of a Roman Catholic?

The Judgment of History

Even historian Will Durant wrote of him that by 1500 (when he was 34 years old), he had "formed his resolve to study and edit the Greek New Testament as the distilled essence of that real Christianity which, in the judgement [sic] of reformers and humanists alike, had been overlaid and concealed by the dogmas, and accretions of centuries."[13]

These facts and others lead us to believe that Erasmus did not believe in the doctrines of the Roman Catholic religion. We see why he worked so hard to find God's preserved words and publish them for all to read. A copy of the second edition of Erasmus' Greek New Testament ended up in a school in Wittenberg, Germany, where a monk named Martin Luther found it. That Greek text helped Martin Luther to start the Reformation, which brought us the King James Bible.

Erasmus, who was counted by everyone around him as a Christian, not a Catholic, helped to bring about the resurrection of the preserved Bible (not the Roman Catholic perversion), which in turn helped bring the Protestant Reformation.

Footnotes
[1]Both books are available from Chick Publications.

[2]Gail Riplinger, *In Awe of Thy Word: Understanding the King James Bible, Its Mystery and History, Letter by Letter* (Ararat, Virginia: AV Publications Corp., ©2003). Available from Chick Publications or **www.avpublications.com**

[3]*The New Schaff-Herzog Encyclopedia of Religious Knowledge,* (New York: Funk and Wagnalls, 1909), vol. I., p. 166.

[4]Hastings' *Encyclopedia of Religion and Ethics* (New York: Scribner's, 1928), Vol VI, p. 83.

[5]Owen Chadwick, *A History of Christianity* (New York: St. Martin's Press, 1995), p. 198. Riplinger notes of Erasmus, "He was buried at a Protestant church in Basel" (p. 1).

[6]Roland Bainton, *Erasmus of Christendom* (New York: Scribner's, 1969), pp. 277-278

[7]Will Durant, *The Story of Civilization: The Reformation* (New York: MJF Books, 1957), Vol. 6, p. 437.

[8]Will Durant, *The Story of Civilization: The Reformation,* Vol. 6, p. 285

[9]Will Durant, p. 435

[10]J.A. Froude, *The Life and Letters of Erasmus* (New York: Charles Scribner's Sons, 1894), p. 25.

[11]J.A. Froude, *The Life and Letters of Erasmus,* p. 87.

[12]J.A. Froude, *The Life and Letters of Erasmus*, pp. 260, 356, 118, 349.

[13]Will Durant, *The Story of Civilization: The Reformation,* Vol. 6, p. 273.

QUESTION

What is the *Septuagint*?

ANSWER

If you look in the preface of a modern Bible, you will probably find a reference to the *Septuagint*, or *LXX* for short. The translators of all modern Bibles, including the New King James, use the *Septuagint* along with other texts in translating the Bible. They claim that the *Septuagint* contains true readings not found in the preserved Hebrew text. Thus they give it great importance. But what is the *Septuagint*? Here's how the legend goes:

The *Septuagint* is claimed to have been translated between 285-246 BC during the reign of Ptolemy II Philadelphus of Alexandria, Egypt. His librarian, supposedly Demetrius of Phalerum, persuaded Philadelphus to get a copy of the Hebrew Scriptures. Then the Scriptures (at least Genesis to Deuteronomy) were translated into the Greek language for the Alexandrian Jews. This part of the story comes from early church historian Eusebius (260-339 AD). Scholars then claim that Jesus and His apostles used this Greek Bible instead of the preserved Hebrew text.

The Letter of Aristeas

The whole argument that the Hebrew scriptures were translated into Greek before the time of Christ rests upon a single document. All other historical evidence supporting the argument either quotes or references this single letter.

In this so-called *Letter of Aristeas*, the writer presents himself as a close confidant of king Philadelphus. He claims that he persuaded Eleazar, the high priest, to send with him 72 scholars from Jerusalem to Alexandria, Egypt. There they would translate the Hebrew Scriptures into Greek, forming what we now call the *Septuagint*.

Jewish historian Flavius Josephus, Jewish mystic Philo (both first century AD) and others add to the story. Some say the 72 were shut in separate cells and "miraculously" wrote each of their versions word-for-word the same. They say this proves "divine inspiration" of the entire *Septuagint*.

Thus, the *Septuagint* is claimed to exist at the time of Jesus and the apostles, and that they quoted from it instead of the preserved Hebrew text. This story has been passed around for centuries. But is it the truth? Was this *Septuagint* really written before the earthly ministry of the Lord Jesus and His apostles? Did they quote it? Was it really inspired by God? And if the story is a fake, why make up the story? Is there another reason to get people to use (or believe in) the *Septuagint*?

The Verifiable Facts

•The writer of this letter, Aristeas, claims to have been a Greek court official during the time of Philadelphus' reign. He claims to have been sent by Demetrius to request the best scholars of Israel to bring a copy of the Hebrew scriptures to Alexandria to start the *Septuagint* translation project. He even goes so far as to give names of *Septuagint* scholars, yet many of the names he gives are from the Maccabean era, some 75 years too late. Many of them are Greek names, definitely not the names of Hebrew scholars. There are many other evidences that this letter is from a different time period, and is thus a fake. The writer is lying about his identity.

•The supposed "librarian," Demetrius of Phalerum (ca. 345-283) served in the court of Ptolemy Soter. Demetrius was never the librarian under Philadelphus.

•The letter quotes the king telling Demetrius and the translators, when they arrived, how wonderful it was that they came on the anniversary of his "naval victory over Antigonus" (Aristeas 7:14). But the only such recorded Egyptian naval victory occurred many years after Demetrius death, so the letter is a fraud!

The Letter of Aristeas is a hoax that doesn't even fit the time period in which it claims to have been written. And since the other ancient writers merely add to this story, it is clear that the story itself of a pre-Christian *Septuagint* is a fraud. Even critical textual scholars admit that the letter is a hoax. Yet they persist in quoting the Letter of Aristeas as proof of the existence of the *Septuagint* before Christ.

New Testament Evidence

Many scholars claim that Christ and His apostles used the *Septuagint*, preferring it above the preserved Hebrew text found in the temple and synagogues. But if the Greek *Septuagint* was the Bible Jesus used, he would not have said,

> "For verily I say unto you, Till heaven and earth pass, one jot or one tittle shall in no wise pass from the law, till all be fulfilled." (Matthew 5:18)

Why would Jesus not have said this? Because the jot is a Hebrew letter, and the tittle is a small mark to distinguish between Hebrew letters. If Jesus used the Greek *Septuagint*, His scriptures would not have contained the jot and tittle. He obviously used the Hebrew scriptures!

In addition, Jesus only mentioned the scripture text in two ways, (1) "The Law and the Prophets" and (2) "The Law of Moses, the Prophets and the Psalms":

> "And he said unto them, These are the words which I spake unto you, while I was yet with you, that all things must be fulfilled, which were written in the law of Moses, and in the prophets, and in the psalms, concerning me." (Luke 24:44)

The Hebrews divide their Bible into three parts: the Law, the Prophets and the Writings. Jesus clearly referred to this. The *Septuagint* had no such division. In fact, it contains Apocryphal books interspersed throughout the Old Testament. The sequence is so hopelessly mixed up that Jesus could not possibly have been referring to it!

Who is Pushing the *Septuagint*?

So why do we still hear the story? Why do people give it a second thought? Are there other reasons why they still try to use the *Septuagint* to find "original readings" that were supposedly "lost from the Hebrew"?

1. Roman Catholics Need It

According to the Roman Catholic *Douay* Bible:

> "...the *Septuagint*, the Greek translation from the original Hebrew, and which contained all the writings now found in the Douay version, as it is called, was the version used by the Saviour and his Apostles and by the Church from her infancy, and translated into Latin, known under the title of Latin Vulgate, and ever recognized as the true version of the written word of God" —Preface, 1914 edition.

Roman Catholics desperately want the *Septuagint* to be genuine — even inspired! You see, the so-called *Septuagint* is where they got the Apocrypha (books that are not inspired and have no place in our Bibles). If the *Septuagint* goes, *then the Apocrypha goes with it*!

2. Ecumenical Textual Critics Need It

The supposed text of the *Septuagint* is found today only in certain manuscripts. The main ones are: Codex Sinaiticus (Aleph); Codex Vaticanus (B); and Codex Alexandrinus (A). That's right. The Alexandrian manuscripts are the very texts we call the *Septuagint*!

In his Introduction to *The Septuagint with Apocrypha: Greek and English* (1851) Sir Lancelot Brenton describes how some critical scholars have attempted to call the *Septuagint* by its real name, the Alexandrian Text, but the name never stuck. Thus he admits that they are one and the same.

So we have textual critics who believe desperately in the 44 Alexandrian manuscripts (against more than 5,000 copies favoring the Textus Receptus). They use these to translate all modern New Testaments. But these Alexandrian manuscripts also include the *Septuagint* Old Testament (with the Apocrypha). They have fallen for a trap.

Catholics now argue the following: If you accept the Alexandrian text (which modern scholars use as the basis for all new translations) for your New Testament, then you also have to accept the rest of the Alexandrian text (*Septuagint*) , which includes the Apocrypha. What we are seeing is the development of an ecumenical Bible, including the Apocrypha. Some versions have already gone this way. For many Protestants, all roads are truly leading to Rome.

3. **We Don't Need It**

But do we Christians need the Alexandrian manuscripts? Not at all! For the Old Testament we have the preserved words of God in the Hebrew Masoretic text. For the New Testament we have the 5,000-plus manuscripts in Greek, plus the many early translations spread abroad, to witness to the actual words of Christ and His apostles.

So the *Septuagint* story is a hoax. It was not written before Christ; so it was not used by Jesus or His apostles. It is the only set of manuscripts to include the Apocrypha mixed in with the books of the Bible, so as to justify the Roman Catholic inclusion of them in their Bibles. And it is just those same, perverted Alexandrian codices —the same ones that mess up the New Testament —dressed up in pretty packaging.

Let's stick to our preserved Bible, the King James Bible in English, and leave the Alexandrian perversions alone.

QUESTION

Did Peter quote the Septuagint? In I Peter 1:24-25, Peter quotes Isaiah 40:6-8. But why does it look like he is quoting the Greek Septuagint, and not the Masoretic (Hebrew) verse?

ANSWER

Peter referenced Isaiah 40. But the so-called "*Septuagint*" Old Testament, really written after Peter, was actually changed to quote Peter!

The "Greek *Septuagint*," as you will see in the previous question," really is not what it is claimed to be. It is actually compiled from the "Alexandrian Manuscripts," mainly the Sinaiticus, Vaticanus and Alexandrinus. These big books, or "codices," were written 100-350 years after the New Testament was written. These so-called "scholars" in Alexandria, Egypt included three things in their codices: The Old Testament, translated into Greek; the Apocrypha (non-inspired books that don't belong in a Bible); and at least parts of the New Testament. Their books, with all three parts, looked like a big Roman Catholic Bible. (This is not a coincidence.)

Since people like Origen were putting the Old Testament into Greek 200 years after the New Testament was written, they already knew what Peter, Paul and other New Testament writers said. They had the New Testament right in front of them!

Origen liked the way Peter referenced Isaiah 40:6-8. So when he came to Isaiah 40, he copied Peter's New Testament words right into the *Septuagint* Old Testament! So it is not that the *Septuagint* Old Testament was copied by Peter. The truth is that the *Septuagint*, written after

Peter, copied Peter's style of referring to the Old Testament.

Remember: All the Alexandrian manuscripts, whether New or Old Testament, are a perversion of God's words. They cannot be trusted. But you can trust your King James Bible as God's preserved words in English.

QUESTION

Why did the KJV translators refer to "Saint" Luke? Isn't that Catholic?

ANSWER

Are you a saint? I am. I am a believer. Paul called all believers "saints:"

- Rome: "called to be **saints**" (Romans 1:7)
- Corinth: "called to be **saints**" (1 Corinthians 1:2; see also 2 Corinthians 1:1)
- Ephesus: "to the **saints**" (Ephesians 1:1)
- Philippi: "to all the **saints**" (Philippians 1:1)
- Colosse: "to the **saints**" (Colossians 1:2)
- To the Hebrews: "all the **saints**" (Hebrews 13:24)

"Saint Luke" is no problem. Just like we say, "brother Luke," it labels Luke as a believer. The Roman Catholic doctrine of "sainthood," meaning someone had a special amount of grace and miracles were attributed to them (alive or dead), came centuries later. The term, "Saint Luke," lines right up with New Testament doctrine and is perfectly appropriate in the King James Bible.

Chapter 3

Is The King James Bible Translated Correctly?

Questions about the Godhead

QUESTION

Why doesn't the King James Bible always translate "Yahweh" as Jehovah?

ANSWER

You expressed a concern about the following statement by Gail Riplinger:

> "Now we are seeing a parallel move within the new Bible versions where it's not Jehovah anymore it's just 'Lord.' It's not Jesus Christ it is just 'the Christ.'"

You are correct that the KJV uses "LORD" to translate the divine name in most instances. However, there are seven instances in which the KJV translators used "Jehovah" for very specific reasons. Gail Riplinger was correct that modern Bibles have removed "Jehovah" in these seven instances. The KJV translators used the name "Jehovah" whenever the name Yahweh was found under one of the following three conditions:

1. When YHWH is used as God's personal name.

> **Exodus 6:3** And I appeared unto Abraham, unto Isaac, and unto Jacob, by the name of God

Almighty, but by <u>my name</u> JEHOVAH was I not known to them.

Psalm 83:18 That men may know that thou, <u>whose name alone</u> is JEHOVAH, art the most high over all the earth.

2. When God's name is repeated as "Jah Jehovah."

Isaiah 12:2 Behold, God is my salvation; I will trust, and not be afraid: for the LORD JEHOVAH is my strength and my song; he also is become my salvation.

Isaiah 26:4 Trust ye in the LORD for ever: for in the LORD JEHOVAH is everlasting strength:

3. When God's personal name is part of a place name.

Jehovah-jireh

> **Genesis 22:14** And Abraham called <u>the name of that place</u> Jehovah-jireh: as it is said to this day, In the mount of the LORD it shall be seen.

Jehovah-nissi

> **Exodus 17:15** And Moses built an altar, and called <u>the name of it</u> Jehovah-nissi:

Jehovah-shalom

> **Judges 6:24** Then Gideon built an altar there unto the LORD, and <u>called it</u> Jehovah-shalom: unto this day it is yet in Ophrah of the Abiezrites.

Jehovah was the pronunciation of JHVH (YHWH) that the English speaking people understood as the Personal Name of God. So in places where the Personal Name of God was emphasized, the King James translators transliterated the Name Jehovah.

Jehovah or Yahweh?

While I am sure that God does not care whether we pronounce His personal Name as Jehovah or Yahweh, even the New American Standard translators admit that "It is known that for many years YHWH has been transliterated as Yahweh, however no complete certainty attaches to this pronunciation" (Principles of Translation from the "Preface to the New American Standard Bible," 1997 edition). The pronunciation is a moot point.

If the vowels added later in Hebrew (200-700 AD by the Massoretes) are not the way to pronounce the Name of God, then there is nowhere that we can find the correct pronunciation. Many modernist "scholars" say that Yahweh was a local god that was elevated by the tribe of Israelites to the One God. They say Yahweh was the consort (lover) god of Baal, maybe even female! But if you say "Jehovah" (like when you say "hell" instead of "sheol") people know what you are talking about: the One Personal, Invisible God of Israel and the Christian Church.

Gail Riplinger has a point. Something as clear and meaningful as this has been stripped of its significance by the generic word "LORD" or "GOD" in these seven instances. Just because the modern bibles (including the NKJV) changed it does not mean they IMPROVED it.

The King James translators understood, as our modernist translators do not, that there was significance in these seven places where the personal name of God was referred to. They transliterated JHVH as Jehovah only in these places, for these good reasons. The modernists have once again simply decided to hide these significant points from the reader.

QUESTION

Why does the KJV use the term "God forbid" when the Greek word for God, *theos*, does not appear in any Greek manuscript of the *Textus Receptus* family?

ANSWER

Mee genoito, "May it not (never) be" is an extreme saying. It is like saying, "May it never ever happen!" It is stated in a passive form, but the meaning is actually more along these lines, "May God never let that happen."

This is especially true since God is the one superintending over what does and does not happen on earth. That is why "God forbid!" is an excellent and accurate translation both of the meaning and of the intensity of *mee genoito*.

QUESTION

Why does Romans 8:16, 26 refer to the Holy Spirit as an "it" and not a "he"?

ANSWER

The King James translators were honest and had one goal: to communicate God's own words in the English language. When they read the Greek, they saw the Holy Ghost is referred to in the neuter, not masculine or feminine. In English, the only way to legitimately translate the neuter is to say "it."

Which do you really want: a translation that gives you what the translators think God really meant (as if He could make a mistake), or a translation that actually puts in your language exactly what God really said? I want God's exact words in my language, not man's counterfeit guesses. I trust that the Holy Spirit is able to teach me what they mean.

QUESTION

Why is the word in Hebrew for the Holy Spirit a female noun? I am not saying God is a woman or a man. I am saying the word for Holy Spirit in Hebrew is of feminine gender.

ANSWER

Gender in a noun does not always mean it is referring to a male or a female.

Most words in non-English languages have gender. If in Spanish the word for "fish" is masculine (*pescado*), does it only refer to a male fish? No, of course not. It just means that the word for fish is expressed in the masculine gender. We English-speakers have taken out many of the gender markers on words. Other than words like "steward" vs. "stewardess," most English words have no gender.

The Hebrew word for spirit, *ruach*, is a feminine noun. But that simply means the word itself is expressed in that gender. Nothing more is implied.

It does not indicate that the Holy Spirit is feminine. It is simply the way that word is rendered in that language. In the Greek language of the New Testament, the word for "spirit" is pneuma, which is a neuter noun. Basing a doctrine on the gender of a noun in Hebrew or Greek is sheer foolishness.

Questions about the Birth of Christ

QUESTION

Which is correct in 1 Timothy 3:16, "God was manifest in the flesh" (KJV) or "He appeared in a body" (NIV)?

ANSWER

Without a doubt, the Scripture says, "God was manifest in the flesh." The vast testimony of history shows us clearly that the word in question is "God," not "he" or "who." But the Alexandrian lie ended up even in the Roman Catholic Vulgate and all modern perversions. Here's how easy it was.

In Greek, the word for God was abbreviated, like this:

$$\Theta C$$

But the word "who" (which the NIV called "he") was written like this:

$$O C$$

The *difference* between "God" and "who" in Greek was a little line. The amazing thing is, by the Alexandrians removing a *line* from one letter, they took away the deity of Christ!

The overwhelming testimony of history is that God preserved His words. In thousands of manuscripts, God preserved these words, "God was manifest in the flesh." Though the Roman Catholic religion preserved the perversion of the Alexandrians, and every Alexandrian translation tries to hide it, it is still true: **God was manifest in the flesh.**

You will always find truths like this when you read the King James Bible.

QUESTION

Why did the KJV translators translate *almah* **as "virgin" in Isaiah 7:14?** Some have said that the KJV source actually says, "young woman." If this is so, how did the KJV writers translate it to be "a virgin?"

ANSWER

The KJV translators translated *almah* as "virgin" because that's what it means in the text. Here's why:

First of all, it would not be a "sign" if it said "a young woman will bring forth a child." It's no miracle for a woman to have a baby.

Second, in Matthew 1:23, the Jewish writer Matthew tells us what the prophet said. Writing in Greek, he quoted the Hebrew prophet using a Greek word that can only mean "virgin." I am certain that an apostle of the Lord Jesus Christ, a chosen one of God the Son, inspired by the Holy Ghost, who spoke Hebrew as his native language, would know whether the Hebrew word *almah* should mean "young woman," or what he says, "virgin" (*parthenos*).

Modern so-called "scholars" have tried for years to find ways to disbelieve the Bible. Disbelieving Matthew is certainly a first step I refuse to take.

Which Translation Is Correct?

QUESTION
Should Isaiah 14:12 say "Lucifer" or "morning star?" And does it refer to Satan?

ANSWER
The King James Bible is correct. Although "Lucifer" is the Latin version of the name, the passage is talking about Satan, not a mere Babylonian king.

Light-Bearer or Morning Star?
Throughout the world, if you ask people who *Heyleel* (hey-LEYL) is, most will not know what to answer. But if you ask them, "Who is Lucifer?" you will very likely get the correct answer. People know who Lucifer is. Ask the Luciferians, who worship Lucifer as a being of light. Ask the Satanists, who call their master Lucifer. No one is in doubt as to who Lucifer is.

What if you ask them, "Who is the morning star?" or "Who is the day star?" Most will know it's Jesus. Look at these scriptures:

> **2 Peter 1:19** We have also a more sure word of prophecy; whereunto ye do well that ye take heed, as unto a light that shineth in a dark place, until the day dawn, and the **day star** arise in your hearts:

> **Revelation 22:16** I Jesus have sent mine angel

to testify unto you these things in the churches.
I am the root and the offspring of David, and **the
bright and morning star**.

Any translation that says "day star" or "morning star" or
"star of the morning" in Isaiah 14:12, like most modern
perversions, is bringing confusion. And God is not the
author of confusion (1 Corinthians 14:33). Many people
reading the modern perversions end up asking, "If Lucifer
is the morning star and Jesus is the morning star, then is
Lucifer Jesus?" The modern translations are simply not
clear!

That is not all. The term translated "Lucifer" does NOT
at all mean "morning star" or "star of the morning." That
would be two totally different Hebrew words. The word
means "light-bearer." In Greek it's *heosphoros*, "light-
bearer." In Latin it's translated "Lucifer," light-bearer.
Whether you say *Heyleel*, *heosphoros* or Lucifer, the
meaning is the same: "light-bearer." But only Lucifer
communicates who we are talking about in English.

And not only English uses the term. Look at these
ancient translations of the word. They also use some form
of Lucifer.

Spanish	Reina-Valera (1557 through 1909)	Lucero
Czech	Kralika (1613)	lucifere
Romanian	Cornilescu (to present)	Luceafar

Going Deeper: the Example of Ezekiel

There is evidence that God is speaking through His prophet to someone other than the king, even though it starts out to that person. Ezekiel 28 is an excellent example. It begins by talking about a human being ruling as king of Tyrus (Tyre). Then the scene shifts and the devil behind the leader starts to take focus:

First God addresses the king, called the "prince of Tyrus:"

> **Ezekiel 28:1-2** The word of the LORD came again unto me, saying, Son of man, say unto the prince of Tyrus, Thus saith the Lord GOD; Because thine heart is lifted up, and thou hast said, I am a God, I sit in the seat of God, in the midst of the seas; **yet thou art a man**, and not God, though thou set thine heart as the heart of God

Then to the devil behind the prince, called the "king of Tyrus" (note the more specific references that have nothing to do with the location or time of Tyre):

> **Ezekiel 28:11-17** Moreover the word of the LORD came unto me, saying, Son of man, take up a lamentation upon the king of Tyrus, and say unto him, Thus saith the Lord GOD; **Thou sealest up the sum, full of wisdom, and perfect in beauty. Thou hast been in Eden the garden of God**; every precious stone was thy covering, the sardius, topaz, and the diamond, the beryl, the onyx, and the jasper, the sapphire, the emerald, and the carbuncle, and gold: **the workmanship of thy tabrets and of thy pipes**

was prepared in thee in the day that thou wast created. Thou art the anointed cherub that covereth; and I have set thee so: thou wast upon the holy mountain of God; thou hast walked up and down in the midst of the stones of fire. **Thou wast perfect in thy ways from the day that thou wast created, till iniquity was found in thee.** By the multitude of thy merchandise they have filled the midst of thee with violence, and thou hast sinned: therefore **I will cast thee as profane out of the mountain of God: and I will destroy thee, O covering cherub, from the midst of the stones of fire. Thine heart was lifted up because of thy beauty, thou hast corrupted thy wisdom by reason of thy brightness: I will cast thee to the ground,** I will lay thee before kings, that they may behold thee.

There was no one in Tyre that was in **Eden** or **the mountain of God**. No one there was a cherub (a type of angel). No one there was "**created.**" This is Satan, Lucifer, the serpent, the dragon, the devil. (I'm sure he recognizes those names for him by now!) Satan/Lucifer/the serpent/the dragon was a cherub, an angel. He was created, since angels were created, not born. Humans were born after Adam and Eve, not created. He was in the garden of God, Eden. He was the "covering cherub." He was "bright" as an angel of light (see also 2 Corinthians 11:14).

Now let's look back at Isaiah 14. Isaiah also begins talking to the physical king of Babylon, then afterward to the spirit behind him.

It starts out to the king:

Isaiah 14:4-8 …thou shalt take up this proverb against the king of Babylon, and say, How hath the oppressor ceased! the golden city ceased! The LORD hath broken the staff of the wicked, and the sceptre of the rulers. He who smote the people in wrath with a continual stroke, he that ruled the nations in anger, is persecuted, and none hindereth. The whole earth is at rest, and is quiet: they break forth into singing. Yea, the fir trees rejoice at thee, and the cedars of Lebanon, saying, Since thou art laid down, no feller is come up against us

Then it changes in tone:

Isaiah 14:12-15 How **art thou fallen from heaven,** O Lucifer, son of the morning! how art thou cut down to the ground, which didst weaken the nations! **For thou hast said** in thine heart, **I will ascend into heaven, I will exalt my throne above the stars of God: I will sit also upon the mount of the congregation**, in the sides of the north: **I will ascend above the heights of the clouds; I will be like the most High**. Yet thou shalt be brought down to hell, to the sides of the pit.

The scriptures tell us who this is. Jesus said:

Luke 10:18-20 And he said unto them, **I beheld Satan as lightning fall from heaven**. Behold, I give unto you power to tread on serpents and scorpions, and over all the power of the enemy:

and nothing shall by any means hurt you. Notwithstanding in this rejoice not, that the spirits are subject unto you; but rather rejoice, because your names are written in heaven.

Revelation also leaves no doubt as to who fell from heaven:

> **Revelation 12:7-12** And there **was war in heaven: Michael and his angels fought against the dragon**; and the dragon fought and his angels, And prevailed not; neither was their place found any more in heaven. **And the great dragon was cast out, that old serpent, called the Devil, and Satan, which deceiveth the whole world: he was cast out into the earth, and his angels were cast out with him.** And I heard a loud voice saying in heaven, Now is come salvation, and strength, and the kingdom of our God, and the power of his Christ: for the accuser of our brethren is cast down, which accused them before our God day and night. And they overcame him by the blood of the Lamb, and by the word of their testimony; and they loved not their lives unto the death. Therefore rejoice, ye heavens, and ye that dwell in them. Woe to the inhabiters of the earth and of the sea! for the devil is come down unto you, having great wrath, because he knoweth that he hath but a short time.

So we know that the only ones in the Bible that fell from heaven are the Devil and his angels. These are the ones for whom "everlasting fire," the lake of fire, was made:

Matthew 25:41 Then shall he say also unto them on the left hand, Depart from me, ye cursed, into everlasting fire, prepared for the devil and his angels:

Revelation 20:10 And the devil that deceived them was cast into the lake of fire and brimstone, where the beast and the false prophet are, and shall be tormented day and night for ever and ever.

The King James Bible is right, however we view it. Even if we pretend the scripture is only talking **to** the earthly king, it still is clearly talking **about** Satan, the Devil, known world over as Lucifer.

QUESTION

Gehenna is not hell, is it? It was a valley where outcasts, thieves and infected people were thrown when they died. The Bible refers to *Gehenna* as the place of death and pain. The word "hell", as you so often use, where eternal pain and fire awaits, is actually *Gehenna*. If you have read a bible written before 1400, you will notice a very important fact: "HELL" is missing. Instead it says *Gehenna*. There is no fire breathing eternal pain demon hell!! In fact YOU are committing a sin here. Telling people, or lying to people about hell, when you should know about *Gehenna*. There is no hell. Only the valley of *Gehenna*. A graveyard!!

ANSWER

The word *Gehenna* is properly translated "hell" in the King James Bible. And actually, except for three known Bibles[1], every Bible says "hell," not the untranslated word *Gehenna*.

What Does *Gehenna* Mean?

Gehenna originally referred to the Valley of Hinnom by Jerusalem. It was the place of horrible idolatry. So when the Hebrews finally came back to Jerusalem after 70 years of Babylonian Captivity (about 605-535/6 BC), they resolved never to use the Valley of Hinnom for idolatry again. Instead, they burned their trash there, and it became a burning valley of waste.

But we know that Jesus and the apostles didn't mean to refer to a garbage dump. Here's why. There are certain statements in the Bible that tell us clearly about *Gehenna*, translated "hell" in the King James Bible. Notice these verses.

Both Body and Soul are Destroyed There

Matthew 10:28 And fear not them which kill the body, but are not able to kill the soul: but rather **fear him which is able to destroy both soul and body in <u>hell</u>**.

No power on earth can destroy a soul. The soul is a part of a person that exists beyond physical death (Revelation 20:4). *Gehenna* has to be a place to destroy both the body **and the soul**.

A Person Goes There After Death

Luke 12:4-5 And I say unto you my friends, Be not afraid of them that kill the body, and after that have no more that they can do. But I will forewarn you whom ye shall fear: Fear him, which **after he hath killed hath power to cast into hell**; yea, I say unto you, Fear him.

It is no threat to throw a dead body into a grave, a junkyard or a furnace. But God has power to cast a person, whose body is dead, into "*Gehenna*." There is only one reason to fear the person that can throw you into *Gehenna*: you must be aware that you are cast there. So *Gehenna* is hell, the place where the unrighteous dead are cast.

Its Fire Shall Never be Quenched

Mark 9:43, 45 And if thy hand offend thee, cut it off: it is better for thee to enter into life maimed, than having two hands **to go into <u>hell</u>, into the fire that never shall be quenched**:

Gehenna is said to be a "fire that shall never be quenched." The earth and the works therein shall all be burned up (2 Peter 3:10), but they will be replaced with a new earth wherein righteousness dwells (2 Peter 3:13; Revelation 21:1). So *Gehenna* could not mean an earthly place, since all fires shall be quenched on earth. But hell's fire shall never be quenched. It is clear: *Gehenna* is hell, not a trash dump.

Even though the word *Gehenna* comes from the Valley of Hinnom, simply rendering it as "garbage dump" or "valley of waste disposal" or "burning garbage" could not be an accurate translation, because that's not what Jesus and the apostles **meant** when they used the word. It meant "the place where people go when they die." That's what we mean when we say "hell."

You wrote:

> If you have read a bible written before 1400, you will notice a very important thing, HELL is missing. Instead it says *Gehenna*.

You mentioned Bibles before 1400. The only known Bible in English from before then is the Wycliffe Bible of 1380. Does it use "hell" or *Gehenna*? Let's find out!

The term *Gehenna* is found in Greek in these verses of the Bible:

Matthew 5:22,29-30; 10:28; 18:9; 23:15,33; Mark 9:43,45,47; Luke 12:5; James 3:6

Here they are in the Wycliffe version:

> **Matthew 5:22** But Y seie to you, that ech man that is wrooth to his brothir, schal be gilti to doom; and he that seith to his brother, Fy! schal be gilti to the counseil; but he that seith, Fool, schal be gilti to the fier of **helle**.

Matthew 5:29-30 That if thi riyt iye sclaundre thee, pulle hym out, and caste fro thee; for it spedith to thee, that oon of thi membris perische, than that al thi bodi go in to **helle**. And if thi riyt hond sclaundre thee, kitte hym aweye, and caste fro thee; for it spedith to thee that oon of thi membris perische, than that al thi bodi go in to **helle**.

Matthew 10:28 And nyle ye drede hem that sleen the bodi; for thei moun not sle the soule; but rather drede ye hym, that mai lese bothe soule and bodi in to **helle**.

Matthew 18:9 And if thin iye sclaundre thee, pulle it out, and caste awei fro thee. It is betere to thee with oon iye to entre in to lijf, thanne hauynge tweyn iyen to be sent in to the fier of **helle**.

Matthew 23:15 Wo to you, scribis and Farisees, ypocritis, that goon aboute the see and the loond, to make o prosilite; and whanne he is maad, ye maken hym a sone of **helle**, double more than ye ben.

Matthew 23:33 Ye eddris, and eddris briddis, hou schulen ye fle fro the doom of **helle**?

Mark 9:43 (9:42) And if thin hoond sclaundre thee, kitte it awey; it is betere to thee to entre feble in to lijf, than haue two hondis, and go in to **helle**, in to fier that neuer schal be quenchid,

Mark 9:45 (9:44) And if thi foote sclaundre thee, kitte it of; it is betere to thee to entre crokid in to euerlastynge lijf, than haue twei feet, and be sent in **helle** of fier, that neuer schal be quenchid,

Mark 9:47 (9:46) That if thin iye sclaundre thee, cast it out; it is betere to thee to entre gogil iyed in to the reume of God, than haue twey iyen, and be sent in to **helle** of fier, where the worme of hem dieth not,

Luke 12:5 But Y schal schewe to you, whom ye schulen drede; drede ye hym, that aftir he hath slayn, he hath power to sende in to **helle**. And so Y seie to you, drede ye hym.

James 3:6 And oure tunge is fier, the vniuersite of wickidnesse. The tunge is ordeyned in oure membris, which defoulith al the bodi; and it is enflawmed of **helle**, and enflawmeth the wheel of oure birthe.

So you see that *Gehenna* is **not** the term used in English at all! Not until Young's Literal Translation in the late 1800s, followed by the Catholic New American Bible of 1970 was the untranslated *Gehenna* put in. Look at foreign translations. The Spanish Reina-Valera of 1602-1989 rightly says *el infierno* and the Portuguese Corrigida Fiel says *do inferno*, both of which mean "Hell" as we in English use the term. "Hell" is an understandable word. *Gehenna* is not.

And "hell" accurately translates the meaning of the word *Gehenna*. *Gehenna* is not a translation; it is just a transliteration (translating letters, but not meaning). We find that first in the perverted Roman Catholic Latin Vulgate (400s AD), which was forced on the people of

Europe as the only legal Bible for over a thousand years. Not until the Reformation of the 1500s were God's actual words translated into the language of the people. And every one of them was careful to translate *Gehenna* into an English word with the same meaning. All but two of the English Bibles, from at least 1380 onward (that's all I've checked on this so far), translate *Gehenna* into the understandable word "hell."[2] That's what a good Bible should do.

You are welcome to read the article "Who Needs Hell?"[3] It will show you why it is important to translate the word into a word that makes sense in English.

Footnotes

[1]Specifically, the Roman Catholic Latin Vulgate (400s AD), Young's Literal Translation (1862 & 1898) and the Roman Catholic New American Bible (1970-1991)

[2]This list includes the 1380 Wycliffe, the 1534 & 1535 Tyndale, the Cranmer (Great) Bible of 1539 & 1540, the Geneva Bibles of 1557, 1560 and 1599, the Bishop's Bible of 1568 & 1602, even the Jesuit Rheims New Testament of 1582, and almost all Bibles from 1881 to the present. Except for Young's Literal and the New American Bible, they all say "hell" (spelled "hel," "helle" or "hell"), not *Gehenna*.

[3]This article is found online at http://www.chick.com/information/bibleversions/needhell. asp.

QUESTION

Why should the KJV say "Easter" not "Passover" in Acts 12:4?

ANSWER

"Passover" is not the correct translation of *pascha* in this single New Testament passage. If we examine the Passover celebration and Days of Unleavened Bread from the Old Testament, we will see why Acts 12:4 cannot be about Passover.

When Are the Days of Unleavened Bread?

Here is what the Bible says in Acts 12:1-4:

> Now about that time Herod the king stretched forth his hands to vex certain of the church. And he killed James the brother of John with the sword. And because he saw it pleased the Jews, he proceeded further to take Peter also. (Then were the days of unleavened bread.) And when he had apprehended him, he put him in prison, and delivered him to four quaternions of soldiers to keep him; intending after Easter to bring him forth to the people.

Please note when the apostle James was killed: "Then were the days of unleavened bread." When were those days? The Bible is very specific. In Leviticus 23:5-8 and Numbers 28:16-25 we find two very clear definitions of the days of Passover and the Feast / Days of Unleavened Bread.

- Passover (Hebrew: Pesach) occurs on the 14th day of the first month at even (starting at sunset).
- The Feast and Days of Unleavened Bread start after Passover, on the 15th day of that month (Numbers 28:17) and continuing through the 21st day. Both the

15th and 21st days were treated as Sabbath days, days of worship and not of "servile work" (Lev. 23:7-8; Num. 28:18, 25). The Bible tells us clearly: Passover is before the Days of Unleavened Bread, not after.

What Was Herod Talking About?

A simple summary of the Scriptures will help us understand. The Bible says Herod killed the apostle James (John's brother) with the sword. Then he took the apostle Peter as well. Those days were the Days of Unleavened Bread when he did this. But while Herod wanted to put Peter in front of the people, (intending to kill him with their approval), he decided to wait for something the Greek calls *pascha*. Then he would bring out Peter.

Here is a simple order to keep in mind:

Passover (14 Abib), then Days of Unleavened Bread (15-21 Abib), then *pascha*.

Please note that Passover was before the Days of Unleavened Bread, and this *pascha* Herod was waiting for was after the Days of Unleavened Bread. Therefore while Herod may have been waiting for Easter (the feast of Ishtar[1], which the Greeks also called *pascha*), he was not waiting for Passover. That is why the King James Bible, in this single instance, had to translate *pascha* by a word other than Passover.

The translators of the King James knew their Bible. Do the translators of the modern versions?

Footnotes
[1]Called *Astarte* by the Greeks, and *Ashtoreth* by the Semitic peoples.

QUESTION

Did the King James change "Passover" to "Easter" in Acts 12:4? I have an original 1611 print, handed down through the centuries (see figure 1). In it, Acts 12:4 clearly uses the word "Passover" and not "Easter," as we have it in King James Bibles today. But according to your article[1], revisions to the KJV did not change words, but corrected only spelling and printing errors. If some King James Bibles say "Passover" in Acts 12:4, and other say "Easter," there must have been a revision of the KJV.

ANSWER

The Bible you have is not a King James Bible, but rather a Geneva Bible, printed in 1611 in London by the King's own printer, Robert Barker. Here is how we know.

1. From the text itself

Thank you for scanning the page in your Bible, with Acts 12 circled (see figure 2). It surely does say "Passover"! But if we make a verse by verse comparison (see figure 3) of your Bible with the Geneva Bible and King James Bibles, it becomes clear that what you have is a Geneva Bible.

2. From the cover pages

Here are the cover pages from the three Bibles (figures 4-6). Notice that the cover page of your Bible is very similar to the Geneva Bible, and that the cover page of the third Bible, a KJV, is quite different. Once again, it is clear that the Bible you have is a Geneva Bible.

The Bible that you have appears to be a beautiful example of the Geneva Bible. This one was printed in 1611, the same year as the King James Bible (even by the same printer!). So we can see that the King James never had "Passover." It always said "Easter," from 1611 to the present day. It has never been revised.

Footnotes:
[1]See page 126, "Has the King James Bible been changed between 1611 and today?"

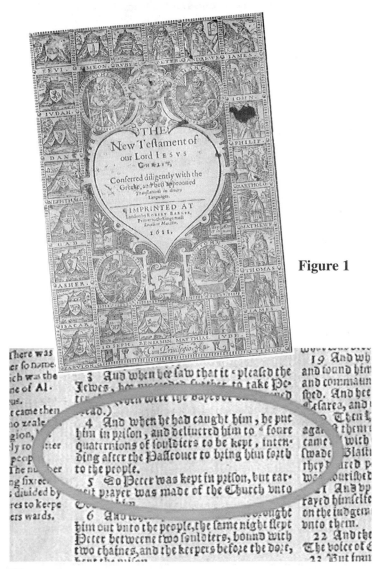

Figure 1

Figure 2

Column one contains verses from this reader's 1611 Bible. Column two contains the same verses from the 1599 Geneva Bible, and column three is from the 1611 King James Bible, in Roman type, a word-for-word copy of the original 1611 printing.

Notice that the words in column one and two are the same (with only minor spelling changes). That's because these are both Geneva Bibles, one printed in 1599 and one printed in 1611. Column three, on the other hand, contains wordings that are different! This is the 1611 King James Bible.

Acts 12 verse	Scan of a "1611 KJV" (1611 Geneva Bible)	1599 Geneva Bible	1611 reproduction KJV
4	And when he had **caught** him, he put him in prifon, and delivered him to foure quaternions of foldiers to be kept, intending after **the Paffeouer** to bring him forth to the people.	And when he had **caught** him, he put him in prifon, and delivered him to foure quaternions of foldiers to be kept, intending after **the Paffeouer** to bring him foorth to the people.	And when he had **apprehended** him, hee put him in prison, and delivered him to foure quaternions of souldiers to keepe him, intending after **Easter** to bring him forth to the people.
7	And behold, the Angel of the Lord came upon **them**, and a light shined in the **houfe**, and hee fmote Peter on the fide, and raifed him up, faying, **Arife** quickly. And his chaines fell off from his hands.	And behold, the Angell of the Lord came upon **them**, and a light fhined in the **houfe**, and he fmote Peter on the fide, and raifed him vp, faying, **Arife** quickly. And his chaines fell off from *his* hands.	And beholde, the Angel of the Lord came vpon **him**, and a light shined in the **prison**: and he smote Peter on the side, and raised him vp, faying, **Arise up** quickly. And his chaines fell off from his hands.

9	So **Peter came** out and followed him, and **knew** not that it was true which was done by the Angel, but thought he **had feene** a vifion.	So *Peter* **came** out and followed him, and **knewe** not that it was true, which was done by the Angel, but thought he **had feene** a vifion.	So **hee went** out, and followed him, and **wist** not that it was true which was done by the Angel: but thought he thought he **saw** a vision.
10	**Nowe when** they were paft the furft and the fecond **watch**, they came vnto the yron gate that leadeth vnto the citie, which opened to them by it owne accord, and they went out, and paffed through one ftreete, and **by and by** the Angel departed from him.	**Now when** they were paft the furft and the fecond **watch**, they came vnto the yron gate that leadeth vnto the citie, which opened to them by it owne accord, and they went out, and paffed through one ftreete, and **by and by** the Angel departed from him.	**When** they were past the first and the second **ward**, they came vnto the yron gate that leadeth vnto the citie, which opened to them by it owne accord: and they went out and passed on thorow one streete, and **forthwith** the Angel departed from him.
11	And when Peter was come to himfelfe, hee fayd, Now I knowe **for a trueth** that the Lord hath fent his Angel, and hath deliuered me out of the hand of Herod, and from all the **waiting for** of the people of the Jewes.	And when Peter was come to himfelfe, he faid, Now I knowe **for a trueth** that the Lord hath fent his Angel, and hath deliuered me out of the hand of Herod, and from all the **waiting for** of the people of the Iewes.	And when Peter was come to himselfe, hee said, Now I knowe **of a suretie,** that the Lord hath fent his Angel, and hath deliuered mee out of the hand of Herode, and from all the **expectation** of the people of the Iewes.

Figure 3

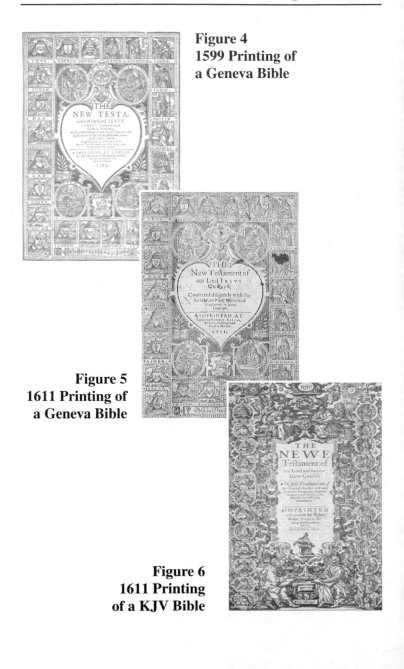

**Figure 4
1599 Printing of
a Geneva Bible**

**Figure 5
1611 Printing of
a Geneva Bible**

**Figure 6
1611 Printing
of a KJV Bible**

QUESTION
Was "not suffer a witch to live" in Exodus 22:18 mistranslated? Should have said "poisoner?"

ANSWER
No, it's not true. The King James Bible is absolutely correct. The words in their widest use simply refer to a witch or a sorcerer. And the ancient languages Akkadian and Ugaritic prove this. Here are two commonly used sources that verify this:

Strong's Concordance
kashaph {kaw-shaf'}, Strong's number 3784.

Meaning: 1) to practice witchcraft or sorcery, use witchcraft 1a) sorcerer, sorceress

Origin: a primitive root; properly, to whisper a spell, i.e. to inchant or practise magic

Theological Wordbook of the Old Testament

1051.0 כָּשַׁף (kāshap) use witchcraft.

(1051a) כֶּשֶׁף (keshep) witchcraft.

(1051b) כַּשָּׁף (kashshāp) sorcerer.

The author of the article writes[1]:

> "This verb and its related nouns mean the same as the Akkadian kašapu and the Ugaritic ktp (sorcery)

> "The pharaoh of the exodus had those who practiced this variety of the occult in his retinue of advisers (Exodus 7:11). They are grouped with the ḥakāmîm (wise men) and ḥarṭummîm (see "magicians").

"These sorcerers were outlawed in Israel. In Exodus 22:17 the feminine form appears m^e kashshēpah and in the long list of Deuteronomy 18:10 the masculine m^e kashēpâ the penalty was death.

"Among the sins of King Manasseh was witchcraft (2 Chronicles 33:6). This is the only occurrence of the finite verb form.

"Another occurrence of the participle is in Daniel 2:2. Like the pharaoh, King Nebuchadnezzar summoned his "sorcerers" along with his "magicians" ḥarṭummîm enchanters (see ʾashshāpîm) and Chaldeans kaśdîm.

"Malachi saw these sorcerers being judged in the end along with adulterers, liars, and oppressors of widows, orphans, and foreigners (Malachi 3:5).

"(keshep) Witchcraft, sorcery, soothsayer, spell. This masculine noun occurs six times in the OT, always in the plural (2 Kings 9:22; Isaiah 47:9, 12; Micah 5:12 [twice in Nahum 3:4]).

"(kashshāp) Occurs only once, Jeremiah 27:9, "sorcerer."

What is the Hebrew Word for Poisoner?

Actually, there is **no** word for "poisoner" in Hebrew. However, there are two words for "poison:"

2534 חֵמָה chemah {khay-maw'}, translated "poison" in Deuteronomy 32:24,33; Job 6:4; Psalm 58:4 and 140:3.

7219 רֹאשׁ ro'sh {roshe}, translated "poison" in Job 20:16 or רוֹאשׁ rowsh {roshe}, translated "gall" in Deuteronomy 29:18; 32:32; Psalm 69:21; Jeremiah 8:14; 9:15; 23:15; Lamentations 3:5, 19 and Amos 6:12.

We do not have to try to find "deeper" meanings in the Greek or Hebrew. God has seen to it that we have a clear translation in His preserved words in English, the King James Bible.

[1]I have edited out or simplified some of the technical words and terms in this article.

QUESTION
When the Ten Commandments say "Thou shalt not kill," does it mean you shouldn't kill at all? Or can you defend yourself, even if you don't kill?

ANSWER
In a big issue like killing another person, it is important to read all the pertinent Scriptures. "Kill" can be used in many different ways:

It can be used of an accidental death, "which killeth any person at unawares" (Numbers 35:11).

It can be used of sacrificing an animal "Then shall he kill the goat of the sin offering, that is for the people" (Leviticus 16:15).

It can be used of death that occurs in a war "If he be able to fight with me (Goliath), and to kill me, then will we be your servants" (1 Samuel 17:9).

It can also be used of a person deciding to kill another, and then doing it (premeditated murder). "And thou shalt speak unto him (Ahab), saying, Thus saith the LORD, Hast thou killed, and also taken possession? And thou shalt speak unto him, saying, Thus saith the LORD, In the place where dogs licked the blood of Naboth shall dogs lick thy blood, even thine" (1 Kings 21:19).

In Exodus 20 and in many places throughout the Old Testament Law (Exodus through Deuteronomy) the word used for "kill" is the Hebrew word *ratsach*, which clearly means "to perform premeditated murder."

The King James Bible does not use bigger words when a smaller one will do. It is obvious from the context (that is, reading more than just this verse where it says "kill") that God is not talking about war, animal sacrifice or accident. He is talking about premeditated murder. We cannot take one small verse and use it alone to decide upon a doctrine. We must read the whole of Scripture.

Thank God we have His accurate, preserved and clearly translated words in the King James Bible. By faithfully reading it, we may find an answer to the difficult questions of life.

QUESTION
Does "replenish" mean "repopulate a world before ours" in Genesis 1:28?

ANSWER
Not at all. To "replenish" something means to "fill" it. So Adam and Eve were told only to "fill" the earth, not "refill" it. We can see this is true in both the dictionary definition and in each of the seven times "replenish" is used in the Bible.

Noah Webster's 1828 Dictionary
In order to understand a classical English word from the King James Bible, we should use a classical English dictionary, like Noah Webster's 1828 dictionary. Here is how it defines the word "replenish:"

> "To fill; to stock with numbers or abundance. The magazines are replenished with corn. The springs are replenished with water. '*Multiply, and replenish the earth,*' Genesis 1."[1]

Seven Bible verses use the word "replenish" or "replenished." Each time it is used in the Bible, it means "fill" or "filled":

1. Replenish (fill) the earth

> **Genesis 1:28** And God blessed them, and God said unto them, Be fruitful, and multiply, and **replenish the earth**, and subdue it: and have dominion over the fish of the sea, and over the fowl of the air, and over every living thing that moveth upon the earth.

> **Genesis 9:1** And God blessed Noah and his

sons, and said unto them, Be fruitful, and multiply, and **replenish the earth**.

God told Adam and Eve to have many children (be fruitful and multiply) and fill (replenish) the earth with people. Then He repeated the same command to Noah and his sons. "Replenish" simply means "fill" both times.

2. Replenished (filled) from the east:

Isaiah 2:6 Therefore thou hast forsaken thy **people the house of Jacob**, because they **be replenished** from the east, and are soothsayers like the Philistines, and they please themselves in the children of strangers.

Here we learn that God's people, "the house of Jacob," were filled (replenished) from the ways of the east. This means they looked to the pagans and adopted their practices.

3. Replenished (filled) every sorrowful soul:

Jeremiah 31:25 For I have satiated the weary soul, and **I have replenished** every sorrowful soul.

The words "satiated" and "replenished" are in a parallel format, saying basically the same thing twice. To "satiate" means to "fill." God tells us that he fills (satiates or replenishes) the weary and sorrowful soul. When we are empty inside, He fills us.

4. Tyrus (Tyre) Replenished (filled) by merchants:

Isaiah 23:2 Be still, **ye inhabitants of the isle**; thou whom **the merchants of Zidon**, that pass over the sea, **have replenished**.

Those who lived on the island-like city of Tyre (or Tyrus) were filled (replenished) with goods from Zidon's (Sidon's) seafaring merchants, who brought their wares from across the Mediterranean Sea.

> **Ezekiel 26:2** Son of man, because that Tyrus hath said against Jerusalem, Aha, she is broken that was the gates of the people: she is turned unto me: **I shall be replenished**, now she is laid waste:

God describes Tyrus as a person that rejoices against the desolation of Jerusalem. Now that Jerusalem "is laid waste," Tyrus expects to be filled (replenished) with either the spoils of war, or from the merchants that will no longer stop in Jerusalem to sell their wares.

> **Ezekiel 27:25** The ships of Tarshish did sing of thee in thy market: and **thou wast replenished**, and made very glorious in the midst of the seas.

The massive trade of the merchants of Tyrus is described in Ezekiel 27:3-24. In verse 25 is the summary. Tyre was filled (replenished) and "made very glorious" among all the nations because of her seafaring merchants.

It is clear from all the above scriptures, "replenish" simply means "fill."

Should we get rid of "replenish"?

Some people think we should replace an "archaic" word like "replenish" with the word "fill." But there is no need. Once you know that "replenish" means "fill," you will never again mistake its meaning. And is the word really archaic? Not at all! Just look at all these "**modern**" Bible versions that **still** use the word "replenish:"

- 1884/1890 Darby
- 1899 Roman Catholic Douay-Rheims
- 1901 American Standard Version (ASV)
- 1917 Jewish Publication Society Old Testament (JPS)
- 1952 Revised Standard Version (RSV)
- 1970-1991 Roman Catholic New American Bible (NAB)
- 1971 The Living Bible (TLB)
- 1982 New King James Version (NKJV)
- 1989 New Revised Standard Version (NRSV)
- 1996 New Living Translation (NLT)
- 2001 English Standard Version (ESV)
- 2001 Edition World English Bible (WEB)

Now we see an amazing fact. "Replenish" is **not even archaic**! It is **still** in use today, and in all but two versions[2], it still means "fill," just as it did when God preserved His words in English in the 1611 King James Bible. Don't "dumb-down" the English language, looking for a "simpler" Bible version. Read, believe and understand what God has used to perfectly translate and preserve His words for us: the King James Bible.

Footnotes:

[1]Webster notes that "replenish" must be a transitive verb to mean "fill." That is, it must be written in the form "replenish something", to mean "fill." And as you saw above in every single instance of "replenish" in the King James Bible, it is used as a "transitive verb. So it means "fill" everywhere you look in your KJV.

[2]The Living Bible and New Living Translation are exceptions. They use "replenish" only one time, and there it means "renew." See the following chart.

	Bible versions that still use the word "replenish to mean "fill":						
Version	Gen. 1:28	Gen. 9:1	Isa. 2:6	Isa. 23:2	Jer. 31:25	Ezek. 26:2	Ezek. 27:25
KJV	√	√	√	√	√	√	√
ASV	√	√		√	√	√	√
DBY				√	√	√	√
DRA							√
ESV					√	√	
JPS	√	√	√	√	√		√
NAB					√		
NKJV					√		
NRSV					√	√	
RSV					√	√	
WEB		√		√	√	√	√

Verses that use "Replenish" to mean "Refill" or "Renew":

TLB   Psa 104:30
NLT   Psa 104:30

As we can see, in all of these Bibles but the Living and New Living, the word "replenish" means "fill" rather than "refill."

QUESTION

Shouldn't "grief" and "sorrows" in Isaiah 53:4 be translated "pain" and "suffering?"

ANSWER

The King James is correct. The Hebrew words have more than one meaning. The KJV translators knew which meaning applied, because they paid close attention to the context in which the words were found. Here is the verse:

> **Isaiah 53:4** Surely he hath borne our **griefs**, and carried our **sorrows**: yet we did esteem him stricken, smitten of God, and afflicted.

Grief and Sickness

The word for "grief" in Hebrew is *choliy*, which can mean "sickness" as we see clearly in Deuteronomy 7:15. In this context the Lord promised health as a blessing of the Old Covenant for obeying Him:

> **Deuteronomy 7:15** And the LORD will take away from thee all **sickness** [Hebrew, *choliy*], and will put none of the evil diseases of Egypt, which thou knowest, upon thee; but will lay them upon all them that hate thee.

But it also rightly means "grief," as we find in Jeremiah, "the weeping prophet":

> **Jeremiah 10:19** Woe is me for my hurt! my wound is **grievous** [Hebrew, *chalah*, a related word]: but I said, Truly this is a **grief** [Hebrew, *choliy*], and I must bear it.

Since "infirmity" is alike in meaning to "sickness," we see God inspired apostle Matthew Levi to translate properly "Himself took our **infirmities** and bare our **sicknesses**. (Matthew 8:17a).

Sorrow and Pain

In the same way, we know the word for **sorrows** [Hebrew, *mak'ob*, also translated **pain**] should be translated the way it is in the King James Bible. Look at these Scriptures, again from "the weeping prophet":

> **Jeremiah 45:3** Thou didst say, Woe is me now! for the LORD hath added grief to my **sorrow** [Hebrew, *mak'ob*]; I fainted in my sighing, and I find no rest.

> **Lamentations 1:12** Is it nothing to you, all ye that pass by? behold, and see if there be any **sorrow** [Hebrew, *mak'ob*] like unto my **sorrow** [Hebrew, *mak'ob*], which is done unto me, wherewith the LORD hath afflicted me in the day of his fierce anger.

The King James Bible is God's preserved words from Greek and Hebrew into English. It is completely and contextually accurate. We need not hesitate to trust exactly what it says, even if we never learn or check the Greek or Hebrew. It's that accurate.

QUESTION

Why does Genesis 42:25 refer to corn, a new world crop? Europeans did not know of its existence until the 16th century. Surely that must be a mistranslation by the KJV translators, because the Jews would have not known about corn.

ANSWER

That is a question most USA citizens would also have. The fact is that the word "corn" comes from a word meaning "grain" and related to "kernel." In the USA, the Native Americans helped the European settlers plant *maiz* (pronounced, "maze") that we later called "corn." Here's some of what Webster wrote on this in his 1828 dictionary:

1. A single seed of certain plants, as wheat, rye, barley and *maiz*; a grain. It is generally applied to edible seeds, which, when ripe, are hard.

2. The seeds of certain plants in general, in bulk or quantity. In this sense, the word comprehends all the kinds of grain which constitute the food of men and horses. In Great Britain, corn is generally applied to wheat, rye, oats and barley. In the United States, it has the same general sense, but by custom, it is appropriated to *maiz*.

Over the years, the residents of the New World used the term corn for *maiz* (or *maize*). All *maiz* is corn, but not all corn is *maiz*. Therefore, the King James Bible is not talking about our *maiz* or corn at all. It is talking of different kinds of grain, specifically wheat, rye or barley.

The King James translators made no mistake 102 times in their translation "corn." It is the New World citizens who mistakenly applied our *maiz* to the Biblical "corn."

Does the KJV Contradict Itself?

QUESTION

Did the dead "wake up in the morning" (Isaiah 37:36) in the King James Bible?

ANSWER

The King James simply translated the Hebrew exactly. Here is the verse in its entirety:

> "Then the angel of the LORD went forth, and smote in the camp of the Assyrians a hundred and fourscore and five thousand: and when they arose early in the morning, behold, they were all dead corpses."

It is obvious from the context of chapters 36 and 37 that it was Hezekiah's men that discovered the Assyrians dead in their camp. Isaiah did not feel the need to add extra words to state the obvious, and neither did the King James translators.

QUESTION

Why do the four gospels attribute three different sentences to Christ as His last? Also, Matthew and Mark say that the last words of Christ were, in Hebrew, "*Eloi, Eloi, lama sabachthani?*" This has traditionally been translated as, "My God, My God, why hast thou forsaken me?" However, a more accurate translation would be, "My El, My El, why has thou forsaken me?" El is the name of a specific pagan god. Why would Jesus call out to a pagan god at the moment of His death?

ANSWER

The Last Words of Christ

"The Last Words of Christ" were not all spoken at one time. They were spoken between 9 am (the third hour of the day, 6 am being the "first hour") and 3 pm (the "ninth hour").

But the "last words" you listed are not His last. Look carefully. I have the four Gospels here. It is the moments before the Lord Jesus "gave up the ghost" that He died:

> **Matthew: 27:50** Jesus, when he had cried again with a loud voice, yielded up the ghost.

> **Mark: 15:37** And Jesus cried with a loud voice, and gave up the ghost.

> **Luke: 23:46** And when Jesus had cried with a loud voice, he said, Father, into thy hands I commend my spirit: and having said thus, he gave up the ghost.

> **John: 19:30** When Jesus therefore had received the vinegar, he said, It is finished: and he bowed his head, and gave up the ghost.

If there is any real issue, it's not in the words spoken over six hours; it's over the words spoken in the last moments of His earthly life. If you notice, Matthew, Mark and Luke all three say that Jesus "cried with a loud voice"

Luke and John both have words Jesus said before he "gave up the ghost." Two sets of them:

"It is finished" and "Father, into thy hands I commend my spirit"

Logically, I can figure which came after which.

First the Lord Jesus said, "It is finished." I have no problem believing that is what He "cried with a loud voice." Can you hear it?

"IT IS FINISHED!!!!"

Then "Father, into thy hands I commend my spirit." He said this to indicate He was GIVING UP His life. Then the Scripture is understood when it says in all four gospels, "he gave up the ghost" (Greek, *ekpneo*, to breath out one's last breath, breathe out one's life).

So there is no conflict. The four gospels are complementary. Each complements the others to give a full picture.

"Eli, Eli, lama sabachthani?"

This is a statement that has precedent. It is a quote of Psalm 22:1, which begins:

Psalm 22:1 "My God, my God, why hast thou forsaken me? why art thou so far from helping me, and from the words of my roaring?" The psalm goes on to describe a lot of things that were fulfilled that day on the cross:

Psalm 22:14 "I am poured out like water, and all my bones are out of joint: my heart is like wax; it is melted in the midst of my bowels." This describes what happens during crucifixion.

Psalm 22:16 "For dogs have compassed me: the assembly of the wicked have inclosed me: they pierced my hands and my feet." Again, this is what happened to the Lord Jesus Christ that day (Luke 24:40; John 20:20, 25).

Psalm 22:18 "They part my garments among them, and cast lots upon my vesture." This again was fulfilled that day, by the soldiers near the cross (witnessed in all four gospels: Matthew 27:35; Mark 15:24; Luke 23:34; John 19:24).

And a wonderful point, that God actually had not rejected His Son is revealed in this psalm:

Psalm 22:23-24 Ye that fear the LORD, praise him; all ye the seed of Jacob, glorify him; and fear him, all ye the seed of Israel. For he hath not despised nor abhorred the affliction of the afflicted; neither hath he hid his face from him; but when he cried unto him, he heard.

"El" was not the name used, in the sense of a pagan deity. "El" was used instead as the name of God. It is found 235 times in the Hebrew Old Testament. Out of those 235 times, 212 times "El" clearly means the one God.

QUESTION
Why are Matthew's and Luke's family trees of Jesus different?

ANSWER
There are two genealogies in the New Testament, Matthew 1:1-17 and Luke 3:23-38. Both of them are accurate. Both are intended to show the Lord Jesus Christ is indeed the Son of David to rule over Israel as its final and eternal King.

The Luke genealogy is that of Mary, and is rather complete. The Matthew genealogy is that of Joseph, and it is arranged for easy memorization and is abbreviated.

Here's why:

Some point out that Hebrew letters also represent numbers, and the name David adds up to fourteen. Regardless, Matthew counts in fourteens for easy memorization or easy reference to Jesus' genealogy through Joseph. The Old Testament provides the names that are in between, except for those after the Babylonian captivity.

Matthew uses this literary device of grouping things in sevens throughout his gospel. Doing that here makes it easier to remember the line leading to Jesus, using what some say is twice the divine number seven, or fourteen. In other words, while Matthew listed some of the main players, generation by generation, he intentionally skipped some generations to make the list easy with fourteens to count three times.

There are other questions regarding using names that are not biological, but legal parents. Matthew uses the custom of the day to list genealogy, not always by father and son, or father and grandson, but sometimes the legal father, ignoring the biological father.

The bottom line is this, Matthew lists Jesus' legal lineage through Joseph, who is not His biological father. But Luke lists Jesus' physical ancestry down to Mary, who literally carried Him in the womb, and thus was His mother.

This all shows that Jesus is the legal and literal Son of David, qualified to reign over Israel.

QUESTION

Why does the KJV state Paul wrote Romans, when Romans 16:22 says Tertius wrote it?

ANSWER

Paul dictated the letter, but Tertius was his scribe.

Let me explain. Business people often have a secretary. They dictate a letter and the secretary writes it. Who wrote the letter?

When you read the bottom it may say something like:
JC/dd

That tells you that the letter was COMPOSED by JC, but typed, or written, by dd. Again I ask, who wrote the letter?

Dd, of course, physically. That is what Tertius did. He physically put pen to papyrus and wrote the physical ink on the physical paper. But the apostle Paul, as it says in Romans 1:1, "Paul, a servant of Jesus Christ, called to be an apostle, separated unto the gospel of God," dictated the letter.

It is the LORD's words to him for the believers in Rome. The letter (epistle) is from Paul, but Tertius acted as the secretary (or "amanuensis") who put pen to paper.

QUESTION

Does the KJV contain contradictions about who are the 12 apostles?

ANSWER

No. The Bible gives us a **clear pattern** so we can know not only who the apostles were, but with what other apostles they were associated. The secret is in the lists of apostles themselves, given clearly in the King James Bible.

Eliminating the Differences

There are four lists. Each shows three groups of four apostles. When grouped, we can see many similarities between them. They answer our questions very simply.

Let's group them up. I've highlighted the words that are the same between all four lists.

Matt. 10:2-4	Mark 3:16-19	Luke 6:13-16	Acts 1:13, 16-19
Simon **Peter, Andrew, James & John**	Simon **Peter, James, John & Andrew**	Simon **Peter, Andrew, James & John**	**Peter, James, John & Andrew**
Philip, Bartholomew, Thomas & Matthew the publican	**Philip, Bartholomew, Matthew & Thomas**	**Philip, Bartholomew, Matthew & Thomas**	**Philip, Thomas, Bartholomew & Matthew**
James son of Alphaeus, Lebbaeus Thaddaeus, **Simon** the Canaanite & **Judas** Iscariot	**James son of Alphaeus,** Thaddaeus, **Simon** the Canaanite & **Judas** Iscariot	**James son of Alphaeus, Simon** Zelotes, Judas brother of James & **Judas** Iscariot	**James son of Alphaeus, Simon** Zelotes & Judas brother of James (**Judas** is dead)

The names that are not exactly the same in all four lists are:

Matt. 10:2-4	Mark 3:16-19	Luke 6:13-16	Acts 1:13, 16-19
Matthew the publican	Matthew	Matthew	Matthew
Lebbaeus Thaddaeus	Thaddaeus	Judas brother of James	Judas brother of James
Simon the Canaanite	Simon the Canaanite	Simon Zelotes	Simon Zelotes
Judas Iscariot	Judas Iscariot	Judas Iscariot	Judas, which was guide to them which took Jesus.

So our differences come down to these:

• It's pretty obvious that Matthew is "Matthew the publican." No problem here.

• Lebbaeus surnamed Thaddeus, is Judas brother of James. "Lebbaeus" means "a man of heart." "Thaddaeus" means "large-hearted" or "courageous." Both were terms of endearment, nicknames of the second apostle named Judas. They are one and the same.

• Simon the Canaanite is Simon Zelotes. The term *Zelotes* means "zealot." "Canaanite" describes where he is from, and Zelotes tells us he was a political zealot. Same guy.

As we can see, these lists do not contradict each other.

Chapter 4

Is the KJV Text Error-Free?

QUESTION

Didn't the KJV add to Scripture in Matthew 27:46? It quotes Jesus as saying *"Eli, eli, lama sabachthani?"* Then it says "that is to say" with the translation behind it. Was it supposed to be written in 2 languages? If it wasn't, would the KJV translators also be guilty of "adding" to the scriptures?

ANSWER

The King James is the accurate text and translation in the English language of God's preserved words, both of Hebrew and Greek.

Here is the scripture in question:

> **Matthew 27:46** And about the ninth hour Jesus cried with a loud voice, saying, Eli, Eli, lama sabachthani? that is to say, My God, my God, why hast thou forsaken me?

The Gospel of Matthew is written in Greek, but Jesus spoke these words in Hebrew. Matthew is giving us the translation of the Hebrew words. The King James Bible translators did not add them.

New Testament writers have done this also in these verses:

> **Matthew 27:33** And when they were come unto a place called Golgotha, **that is to say**, a place of a skull,

Mark 7:11 But ye say, If a man shall say to his father or mother, It is Corban, **that is to say**, a gift, by whatsoever thou mightest be profited by me; he shall be free.

Mark 7:34 And looking up to heaven, he sighed, and saith unto him, Ephphatha, **that is**, Be opened.

Acts 1:19 And it was known unto all the dwellers at Jerusalem; insomuch as that field is called in their proper tongue, Aceldama, **that is to say**, The field of blood.

Luke 23:38 And a superscription also was written over him **in letters of Greek, and Latin, and Hebrew**, THIS IS THE KING OF THE JEWS.

John 19:13 When Pilate therefore heard that saying, he brought Jesus forth, and sat down in the judgment seat in a place that is called the Pavement, **but in the Hebrew**, Gabbatha.

John 19:17 And he bearing his cross went forth into a place called the place of a skull, **which is called in the Hebrew** Golgotha:

Acts 9:36 Now there was at Joppa a certain disciple named Tabitha, **which by interpretation is called** Dorcas: this woman was full of good works and almsdeeds which she did.

Revelation 9:11 And they had a king over them, which is the angel of the bottomless pit, **whose name in the Hebrew tongue is** Abaddon, **but in the Greek tongue hath his name** Apollyon.

When the Bible tells us the meaning of a Hebrew word, that explanation is actually found in the original text. But any time the King James translators felt compelled to add a word for clarity in English, they were honest enough to put it in italics, so we would know that it was not in the original text.

The King James Bible added nothing and took nothing away from God's preserved words. You have no such promise with a perverted, Alexandrian Bible version.

QUESTION

Does 1 John 5:7 belong in the KJV? It's not in any Greek manuscript before 1600, is it?

ANSWER

1 John 5:7 belongs in the King James Bible and was preserved by faithful Christians. But the passage was removed from many Greek manuscripts, because of the problems it seemed to cause.

It is true that there is a small number of Scriptures that are not the same between the King James Bible and the so-called "Majority" Greek text. There are a number of reasons for this:

• The so-called "Majority" text was not really based on the majority of texts, but rather a relatively small number of manuscripts. The last person to try to find the differences between the majority of Greek manuscripts, Dr. von Soden, collated merely 400 of the more than 5,000 Greek texts. In other words, **the so-called "Majority Text" represents less than 8% of the actual Greek manuscripts.** It's not a "majority" at all!

• "Majority" Greek text is also the main Greek text used by the Eastern Orthodox religion. They had a vested interest in changing (or deleting) some texts. More on this in a moment.

• John itself is not in a large number of extant Greek manuscripts.

So why then is 1 John 5:7 in the King James Bible, but not in many of the existing Greek manuscripts? To understand the answer, we must look at the history of what happened shortly after the Bible was written.

The Greek and Roman Institutions

During the early growth of the Christian church, ministers (whether saved or not) wrote down doctrines that they said were Christian and Biblical. Starting after the death of the apostles (about 100 AD) many people taught the lie that Jesus was not God the Son and Son of God, or that Jesus became God at His baptism, or the false doctrine that the Holy Spirit was not God or was not eternal.

After many debates, the growing religion that became known as Roman Catholic eventually agreed on the doctrine of the Trinity. So they had no reason to remove 1 John 5:7 from their Bibles, since it supported what they taught.

A Trail of Evidence

We can find clear mention of 1 John 5:7 through history, from about 200 AD through the 1500s. Here is a useful timeline of references to this verse:

200 AD Tertullian quoted "which three are one" from the verse in his *Apology, Against Praxeas,* chapter 25.

250 AD Cyprian of Carthage, wrote, "And again, of the Father, Son, and Holy Ghost it is written: 'And the three are One'" in his *On The Lapsed, On the Novatians.*[1]

350 AD Priscillian referred to it [Corpus Scriptorum Ecclesiasticorum Latinorum, Academia Litterarum Vindobonensis, vol. xviii, p. 6.]

350 AD Idacius Clarus referred to it [Patrilogiae Cursus Completus, Series Latina by Migne, vol. 62, col. 359.]

350 AD Athanasius referred to it in his *De Incarnatione.*

398 AD Aurelius Augustine used it to defend Trinitarianism in *De Trinitate* against the heresy of Sabellianism.[2]

415 AD Council of Carthage appealed to 1 John 5:7 when debating the Arian belief (Arians didn't believe in the deity of Jesus Christ.)

450-530 AD Several orthodox African writers quoted the verse when defending the doctrine of the Trinity against the gainsaying of the Vandals. These writers are:

A) Vigilius Tapensis in *"Three Witnesses in Heaven."*

B) Victor Vitensis in his *Historia persecutionis* [Corpus Scriptorum Ecclesiasticorum Latinorum, Academia Litterarum Vindobonensis, vol. vii, p. 60.]

C) Fulgentius in *"The Three Heavenly Witnesses"* [Patrilogiae Cursus Completus, Series Latina by Migne, vol. 65, col. 500.]

500 AD Cassiodorus cited it [Patrilogiae Cursus Completus, Series Latina by Migne, vol. 70, col. 1373.]

550 AD Old Latin 2 ms r has it.

550 AD The "Speculum" has it [The Speculum is a treatise that contains some good Old Latin scriptures.]

750 AD Wianburgensis referred to it.

800 AD Jerome's Vulgate has it [It was not in Jerome's original Vulgate, but was brought in about 800 AD from good Old Latin manuscripts.]

1000s AD Miniscule 635 has it.

1150 AD Minuscule ms 88 in the margin.

1300s Miniscule 629 has it.

157-1600s AD Waldensian (that is, Vaudois) Bibles have the verse.

1500 AD ms 61 has the verse.

Even Nestle's 26th edition Greek New Testament, based upon the corrupt Alexandrian text, admits that these and other important manuscripts have the verse: 221 v.l.; 2318 Vulgate [Claromontanus]; 629; 61; 88; 429 v.l.; 636 v.l.; 918; 1; r.

The Greeks were battling a heresy called "Sabellianism[2]" and would have found it easier to combat the heresy by simply removing the troubling passage from their Bibles.

The Vaudois

Now the "Waldensian," or "Vaudois" Bibles stretch from about 157 to the 1600s AD. The fact is, according to John Calvin's successor Theodore Beza, that the Vaudois received the Scriptures from missionaries of Antioch of Syria in the 120s AD and finished translating it into their Latin language by 157 AD. This Bible was passed down from generation to generation, until the Reformation of the 1500s, when the Protestants translated the Vaudois Bible into French, Italian, etc. This Bible carries heavy weight when finding out what God really said. John Wesley[3] and Jonathan Edwards[4] believed, as most of the Reformers, that the Vaudois were the descendants of the true Christians, and that they preserved the Christian faith for the Bible-believing Christians today.

Who Has the Most to Gain?
Who Has the Most to Lose?

The evidence of history shows us that the Roman Catholic religion was relentless in its effort to destroy the Vaudois and their Bible. It took them until the 1650s to finish their hateful attacks. But the Vaudois were successful in preserving God's words to the days of the Reformation.

Now we must ask ourselves: Who had the most to gain by adding to or taking away from the Bible? Did the Vaudois, who were being killed for having their Bibles, have anything to gain by adding to or taking from the words of God? Compromise is what the Roman religion wanted! Had the Vaudois just followed the popes, their lives would have been much easier. But they counted the cost. This was not politics; it was their life and soul. They, above all people, would not want to change a **single letter** of the words they received from Antioch of Syria. And they paid for this with their lives.

What about the "scholars" at Alexandria, Egypt? We already know about them. They could not even make their few 45 manuscripts agree. How could we believe **they** preserved God's words?

The Reformation itself owes a lot to these Christians in the French Alps. They not only preserved the Scriptures, but they show to what lengths God would go to keep His promise (Psalm 12:6-7).

And that's only part of the story about the preservation of God's words.

Footnotes:

[1]**Old Latin**: The Old Latin manuscripts say it this way: *"Quoniam tres sunt, gui testimonium dant in coelo: Pater, Verbum, et Spiritus sanctus: et hi tres unum sunt. Et tres sunt, qui testimonium dant in terra: Spiritus, et aqua, et sanguis: et hi tres unum sunt"* (verses 7-8). This wording (which matches the King James) is similar to that of Cyprian's words in Latin about 250 AD *"Dicit Dominus: 'Ego et Pater unum sumus,' et iterum de Patre et Filio et*

Spiritu sancto scriptum est: 'Et tres unim sunt.' (The Lord says, "I and the Father are One," and again, of the Father, Son, and Holy Ghost it is written: "And the three are One."). (See the online King James Bible preservation lessons by Dr. Thomas D. Holland, Th.D., Lesson 9, Textual Considerations.) Dr. Holland is an excellent scholar that thoroughly discusses the whole issue of the King James Bible and its preservation from the apostles and prophets to the present day. His new book, *Crowned With Glory: The Bible from Ancient Text to Authorized Version* goes into these issues in detail.

[2]**Sabellianism:** Between about 220 and 270 AD, a man named Sabellius taught that the Father, Son and Holy Spirit were identical. People who believed the Father and Son were the same were called Patripassians (Father-sufferers), because they believed the Father and Son were both on the cross. They would use the 1 John 5:7-8 passage to claim that the Trinity was actually the same Person! We can easily see how the Eastern Orthodox would not want any passage of their Bible to say that the Father, Son and Holy Ghost were "one." They would want to emphasize the distinctions between the Trinity and not have 1 John 5:7 in their Bibles. [See *The King James Version Defended*, by Edward F. Hills (Des Moines, Iowa: The Christian Research Press, 1956, 1973) p. 208.]

[3] John Wesley:

John Wesley has this to say about the Vaudois or Waldenses: "It is a vulgar mistake, that the Waldenses were so called from Peter Waldo of Lyons. They were much more ancient than him; and their true name was Vallenses or Vaudois from their inhabiting the valleys of Lucerne and Agrogne. This name, Vallenses, after Waldo appeared about the year 1160, was changed by the Papists into Waldenses, on purpose to represent them as of modern original." (*Notes on the Revelation of John*, Revelation, Chapter 13, Verse 6, p. 936.)

[4]**Jonathan Edwards:**

Here is an important fact cited by Jonathan Edwards: "Some of the popish writers themselves own, that this people never submitted to the church of Rome. One of the popish writers, speaking of the Waldenses, says, The heresy of the Waldenses is the oldest heresy in the world. It is supposed that they first betook themselves to this place among the mountains, to hide themselves from the severity of the heathen persecutions which existed before Constantine the Great. And thus the woman fled into the wilderness from the face of the serpent" (*The Works of Jonathan Edwards* Vol. 4, Work of Redemption., Period 3, From Christ's Resurrection to the End of the World, Part 4, p. 229.)

QUESTION
Why is Mark 16:9-20 omitted or bracketed as not original in most non-KJV Bibles?

ANSWER
Mark 16:9-20 should be in the Bible, <u>since it is found in almost every Bible manuscript of Mark in existence</u>![1]

Overwhelming Evidence
Wherever you look, the evidence, including Alexandrian manuscripts, is over 99% in favor of keeping the words of God in Mark 16:9-20.

Ancient Manuscripts
Out of 620 manuscripts that contain Mark's gospel, <u>only</u> 2 omit the last 12 verses. Here's how it breaks down.

Miniscules (lower-case letter manuscripts):
Out of 600 miniscules that have been investigated, **all 600 miniscules have 16:9-20.**

Uncials or Majuscules (upper-case letter manuscripts):
Out of 15 uncials that have the gospel of Mark, **all 15 uncials have Mark 16:9-20.**

Codices (not a scroll, but in book form):
Out of the five codices that have Mark, **3 out of 5 codices have Mark 16:9-20.** Only the Vaticanus and Sinaiticus remove it. (Some say it was removed *by the same person* in both manuscripts.) But the codices Ephraemi Rescriptus and Bezae have it in its place, as well as Alexandrinus.

That means less than one third of 1% of these cited

manuscripts omit Mark 16:9-20. ONLY TWO! And they're not "better" manuscripts. They're chock-full of errors.

Ancient Church Writings
2nd Century
You can also find Mark 16:9-20 in the 2nd Century Old Latin and Syriac Bibles and the writing of Papias, Justin Martyr, Irenaeus and Tertullian.

3rd to 7th Centuries
It's found in all sorts of other manuscripts and books in the 3rd to 7th centuries, as well. Researcher John William Burgon found *30 early writers* who clearly included Mark 16:9-20.

The Roman Addition
The one other exception to this, and the reason that some Bibles include a "shorter" version of the last verses of Mark, is so phony and Roman that it doesn't need much comment. Here it is:

Perverted Ending to Mark
> And all things whatsoever that had been commanded they explained briefly to **those who were with Peter**; after these things also Jesus Himself appeared and from the east unto the west sent out through them the holy and uncorrupted preaching of eternal salvation. Amen.

This fake verse is inserted after 16:8 or between 16:8 and 16:9 with the real ending included. Emphasis mine.

You can see the early Roman Catholicism coming through, with Peter in the forefront. But the true Bible never does this. He's never exalted above the others. Peter has human frailties like the rest (compare Mark 16:7; Acts 10; Galatians 2:11-21).

A few manuscripts fell for this corruption, as Roman Catholicism began to infiltrate the churches and people began to change the truth of God in their Bibles into a lie (Romans 1:25) to conform to the Roman Religion. But very few manuscripts can be found in any language that have this perversion.

The Truth is Obvious

The Bible SHOULD contain what God said through His inspired apostles and prophets. Any true Bible must contain, without excuse, brackets or footnotes, the entire text of Mark 16:9-20. People may debate what God's preserved words mean, but they have no right to remove God's words from His Bible.

Footnotes:
[1]For more information, read *Final Authority*, by William P. Grady, chapter 5.

QUESTION

Why does the KJV italicize some words? And why don't other versions?

ANSWER

The italics usually are a simple way of telling us when the word in English is not in the Hebrew or the Greek. There is only one exception to this rule, which I will discuss in a moment.

The King James translators had a simple goal: to communicate God's words in the English language. They were quite honest. When the word they needed to communicate the Greek or Hebrew sentence into English was missing, they wrote the word, but in italics. There are two ways in which this happened.

1. The word or words were needed to make sense in English. In 1 John 4 is this verse:

> **1 John 4:3** And every spirit that confesseth not that Jesus Christ is come in the flesh is not of God: and this is that *spirit* of antichrist, whereof ye have heard that it should come; and even now already is it in the world.

It is less clear to write, "and this is that of antichrist." "That what?" you will ask. That *spirit*. To avoid confusion, they supplied in English a word that you could understand from knowing the Greek, but which wasn't directly said in the Bible language.

2. Where the words were in the original, but they didn't have enough evidence at the time. God's help in preservation of His words is found in an unusual way in 1 John 2:23:

Whosoever denieth the Son, the same hath not the Father: *[but] he that acknowledgeth the Son hath the Father also.*

Look at the verse again. This is a bit more complex. The word [but] is not in any manuscript, period. It is needed, however to show the contrast to English readers. That is like the regular italics in the rest of the King James Bible.

But wait! A full 1/2 of this verse is in italics! How could this be? It's simple: the King James translators were very honest. They found some Greek manuscripts at the time that had the verse and others that didn't. But they had enough evidence from other languages that did, and a very good reason why the verse might have been mistakenly removed by a copyist — *homoeoteleuton.*

Homoeoteleuton (ho-moy-oh-<u>tell</u>-you-tahn)
That big Greek word simply means, "having the same ending." The phrase "hath the Father" is at the end of both parts of the verse. In Greek it looks like this: As the copyist looked back and forth between the original and his copy, his eye could have skipped to that same phrase at the end of the verse. Thinking he had already written it, he would have moved on, thus leaving out the last part of this verse.

In order to be truthful, the King James translators included the 2nd half of the verse, because it belongs there. But to be fair with what they had in front of them, they put that 1/2 verse in italics.

The King James Translators Vindicated
But the best part is that history has shown the King James translators correct! As many more minuscule manuscripts (Greek scriptures with all lower-case letters)

were found, many more contained the verse. Of course it was found in many early translations. But in the biggest irony for the King James haters: it was even found in the Alexandrian perversions! The pro-Alexandrian "scholars" could not say the King James translators were wrong, since it even appeared in their own corrupt copies!

The Bottom Line

The main point is this: God made sure the King James Bible was not only an accurate and excellent translation of His words in English, He even made sure they were quite honest in their use of italics. Some have even gone so far as to say, "even the italics are inspired." What I will conclude is this: God watched over every word of His Bible in English, the King James Bible (or Authorized Version), to be sure we would have God's preserved words in our powerful and influential language. And this has been confirmed time and again, every time I research what is in the King James Bible.

QUESTION

Why are Jesus' words "For thine is the kingdom, and the power, and the glory forever. Amen" found in Matthew but not Luke?

ANSWER

One reason God preserved His words, not just His "word" in general is because every single word is very important — to God and to us. When we look at the context of each Scripture, the answer to the differences between Matthew's and Luke's recording of the Lord's prayer becomes clear. Remember as you read that the terms of **location** and **direction** (up, down, into, out of) are very literally true.

The Context of Matthew

The time Matthew quotes Jesus' prayer is **during the Sermon on the Mount** (recorded in Matthew 5-7). Jesus was speaking to multitudes who came to hear Him. We find this proof in Matthew 5:1-2:

> And seeing the multitudes, **he went up into a mountain**: and when he was set, his disciples came unto him: And he opened his mouth, and taught them, saying,"

After Jesus spoke what we find in Matthew during this sermon, He, His disciples and a multitude of people descended from the mountain. We find this at the beginning of chapter 8:

> **Matthew 8:1** When he was come down from the mountain, great multitudes followed him.

Two chapters later, Jesus commissioned His twelve disciples and called them apostles (Matthew 10:1-42).

The Context of Luke

However it is a different **time** and **place** where Jesus said a similar prayer in Luke. Jesus had already commissioned His twelve apostles in 6:13-16. That means it is later in time than Matthew's Sermon on the Mount. After this commissioning, the Lord Jesus Christ **came down from a mountain** (Luke 6:12, 17), not up into a mountain, with His apostles and other followers to a **plain** to speak to them. In Luke 10:1-24, Jesus Christ commissioned 70 others to heal and preach as well. Then in Luke 11:1, we read these words:

> And it came to pass, that, as he was praying in a certain place, when he ceased, one of his disciples said unto him, Lord, teach us to pray, as John also taught his disciples.

Note two differences: 1) Jesus was praying in a certain place, not preaching to a multitude; 2) When He was finished, one of His disciples asked Him directly to teach them how to pray.

The differences between the two occurrences of the "Lord's Prayer" (really the "Disciples' Prayer") are perfectly explained by the fact that they were said on two completely different occasions, with two different audiences, and for different reasons.

That is nothing like the issue of the Alexandrian perversions removing God's actual words from the pages of Scripture. It is simply the exact words the Lord Jesus Christ said on two different occasions.

QUESTION

If my Bible quotes a non-biblical source, does that mean the source is true?

I have been reading lately about how the Bible contains quotes from extracanonical texts as in Acts 17:28. Even the Old Testament quotes from rabbinical texts, right? Do you feel that these texts should have been omitted from the canon? Why would Jude quote from "The Assumption of Moses" in Jude 9 and then "The Book of Enoch" in Jude 14 if they are now considered 'apocryphal'?

ANSWER

I have a fundamental faith regarding the scriptures. God 'superintended' the texts, so that what God wanted in there is in there, and what God didn't want in there isn't. That means that if God through Paul quotes Epimenides in Titus 1:12, and summarizes the writing of Aratus and Cleanthes in Acts 17:28, it's only there because the quote itself states what the Biblical author wanted to say. It does not validate the entire writings of non-inspired authors.

The same is true with the apocryphal (kept out of the Canon by God) Assumption of Moses and 2 Enoch. Those words say what the Bible author wanted to say. It does not say that the entire writings are therefore God's words.

QUESTION
Has the King James Bible been changed between 1611 and today?

ANSWER
There have only been two modifications of the King James Bible: correction of printing errors and changes in the English language itself.

Printing Corrections
Typesetting in the 1600s was a very laborious task. Each letter on each page had to be put into place. Since there are 3,566,480 letters in the Bible, that leaves a lot of room for mistakes. But in 1628, only 27 years after the first editions of the Bible were printed, 72% of the around 400 printing corrections were already accomplished. By 1850 all corrections of printing errors were made (with the exception of two which shall be detailed below).

Changes in the English Language
The King James Bible was originally printed in Gothic type. That means "v" looked like "u," "J" looked like "I," and there was an "s" that appeared in certain words that looked a little like our "f." So "Iefvs" in Gothic type was the same as "Jesus" in Roman type. The Bibles we read now are in Roman type. Changing the type from Gothic to Roman has been labeled by some as a "change," but it really is not. The words themselves were not changed, only the way the letters were written.

But the spelling of words also changed. By the 1800s, "wee" was "we, "fheepe" was "sheep," "sayth" was "saith," and "euill" was "evil." But those spellings are not difficult. You can figure out what the words said, even from a 1611 copy.

Textual Changes

This is a very important point —**there was not a single textual change in the King James Bible.** But the New King James (NJKV) is a different story. The NKJV is not a true King James Bible. The NKJV publishers used different manuscripts and introduced completely different meanings into their texts. They did not stay with the accurate, preserved meanings of Hebrew and Greek words you find in your King James Bible. They switched words to be what you find in a NIV, NASV or RSV. I will say it again: the King James Bible has no textual changes in any edition, whatsoever.

Two Current Mistakes in Some KJVs

There are actually two single mistakes that were introduced by printers at Oxford University Press over 60 years after the KJV was first printed. They are in 2 Chronicles 33:19, where it says "sins" instead of "sin," and Jeremiah 34:16, where they mistakenly printed "whom he" instead of the correct "whom ye." Both of these were originally translated correctly. But Oxford printers made these two mistakes. Cambridge University Press did not make the printing error. And all Cambridge-type texts have the correct readings. But some publishers misprint one or the other verse in their Bibles. Amazingly, the New King James also has *the same Oxford mistake* in Jeremiah 34:16!

Put to the Test

In the 1850s, after the typographical corrections and spelling changes were completed in the King James, the American Bible Society wrote two reports on the present condition of the English Bible[1]. The second report stated:

"[The] English Bible as left by the translators has come down to us unaltered in respect to its text."

The simple fact is that the King James Bible you can purchase in almost any bookstore, allowing for changes in spelling (and possibly the two printing errors), is the same Book of God's preserved words that was printed in 1611. We can thank God for that.

Footnotes:

[1]In 1852 the American Bible Society wrote Committee on Versions to the Board of Managers. In 1858 a second report was written, Report of the Committee on Versions to the Board of Managers of the American Bible Society. This information can be found Dr. Thomas Holland's book, *Crowned with Glory: The Bible from Ancient Text to the Authorized Version*, p. 101.

QUESTION

Do all publishing companies publish "the same" identical King James Bible?

ANSWER

No. All KJVs are not the same. The best text is the Cambridge KJV. Here's why.

Two Kinds of Changes

As I mentioned in the previous question, there have been only two changes in the KJV text from 1611 to today: 1) spelling errors corrected and 2) spelling changes made to match changes in the English language. Other editions of the KJV, printed by different publishers, have slight differences that are not what the pure King James text says.

Slight Differences

Many publishers, large and small, such as those that made family Bibles between the 1800s and 1900s, did not use the Cambridge text as the standard. These people sometimes spelled a few words differently, or substituted one word for another, such as "always" where the KJV says "alway." (See Numbers 9:16; Deuteronomy 11:1; 2 Kings 8:19, etc.). Of course, the most obvious change in text is the Oxford error: wrongly putting "sins" for "sin" (2 Chronicles 33:19) and "he" for "ye" (Jeremiah 34:16). But even these slight differences in the worst copies of the KJV are far better than the "best" readings in the Alexandrian perversions!

The Best Kind of KJV

The only KJV I completely trust is the Cambridge-type. Those Bibles that use that exact Cambridge text, such as most Cambridge KJV Bibles, and the *Prophecy Study Bible*[1], are what you want. This is the only way to be sure you have an absolutely correct King James Bible. That's what I use and that's what I recommend.

Footnotes:
[1]The proper name is the "Tim LaHaye Prophecy Study Bible." But I do not believe a man's name should be on a Bible, so I do not refer to it by its full name.

Chapter 5

What's Wrong with the Other Versions?

Missing Words

QUESTION
Is the Lord's Prayer in your Bible?

ANSWER
A century after Christ there was a man named Marcion. He pretended to be a Christian, but his beliefs did not match the Bible. He did not believe in God the Father and God the Son (the Lord Jesus Christ). He taught people that there was an evil "creator/warrior god" of the Old Testament, and a nice, "good-guy god" of the New Testament.

But the Bible is clear about the Godhead. So Marcion decided to remove what he didn't like from the gospel of Luke. One passage he changed was the Lord's Prayer, found in Luke 11:2-4. The words in bold are the words Marcion took out:

> And he said unto them, When ye pray, say, **[Our]** Father **[which art in heaven]**, Hallowed be thy name. Thy kingdom come. **[Thy will be done, as in heaven, so in earth]**. Give us day by day our daily bread. And forgive us our sins; for we also forgive every one that is indebted to us. And lead us not into temptation; **[but deliver us from evil]**.

Even a Satanist or other occultist can pray Marcion's

prayer, because it leaves out the Father in heaven. People can fill in the blank as they wish. "Father" is a term used by Buddhists, occultists, and even Satanists. But there is only one "**Father which art in heaven**."

Get out an NIV or other so-called "modern" version. There, in Luke 11, is Marcion's mutilated prayer! When the Alexandrian "scholars" were making their own perversion of the Scriptures, they used Marcion's words, not the Lord's.

If *that* is in your Bible, *what else is in there?*

QUESTION

Does what's missing matter? It's true that my Bible is *lacking* phrases of the Lord's prayer in Luke. But this fact does not discount the validity of the entire translation. In fact, Matthew 6:9-13 contains a more complete version of Jesus' prayer.

I do not argue that Luke's version in the NIV may resemble Marcion's version of the Lord's prayer[1]. But I am concerned that you seem to discredit other translations of the Bible solely on the fact that certain clauses are *not found* in specific scripture passages.

I think that it is important to remember that the Bible should be understood as a complete work, the Word of God, and that no one passage should be extracted and used as the sole base for doctrine.

ANSWER

There is a key here. Please notice the words "*lacking*" and "*not found*." God said "My words shall not pass away" (Mark 13:31) and "thou shalt preserve them (God's words) from this generation for ever" (Psalm 12:7).

Since God promised to preserve His words, it should arouse our curiosity when we find that words, phrases, even whole verses are missing from the Bible[2].

Here are some important points to consider:

How do "scholars" decide when to remove a verse from the Bible?

The Bible revisers are carving up the Bible based on a mere 44 or so manuscripts, which disagree with over 5,000 copies of the Scriptures. If a modern scholar finds one single manuscript that does not have a word or verse found in the King James Bible, he often removes it on that basis alone, (unless he likes the verse, of course). Other of his favorite texts may actually have the word or verse. So if he wants to get rid of it, he simply picks the text that removes it. If this sounds arbitrary, it is. Critics simply pick and choose their favorite reading. That's what you do when you ignore the broad evidence of history.

Then how do we know when to stop?

The biggest temptation is to keep removing verses until we feel that what's left is the truth. On what basis? Our own feelings. Over 95% of all the manuscripts support the King James. New Bibles are alike in that they intentionally leave out most of the same words, phrases and verses.

Finally, as you keep removing words from verses about vital doctrines (the godhead, trinity, salvation, Jesus Christ as God, hell, fasting, prayer, adultery, sodomy, etc.) **you will have a problem**. God repeats Himself to emphasize vital doctrines. Modern Bibles take away many places where God says the same thing again. Thus modern Bibles make it look like those doctrines weren't so important to God.

My Hebrew professor in a "conservative Evangelical" seminary taught us that if anything was not repeated in the Bible, it was not true! He was willing to doubt historical facts not found in more than one place in the Bible.

In the letter above is this statement: "no one passage should be extracted and used as the sole base for doctrine." The modern, Alexandrian-based Bibles make it even worse: they knock down the number of times God teaches us important doctrines.

Ask yourself

Do you want a Bible that has been shortened by men, or the complete one that is inspired by God?

Footnotes:

[1]See page 131, Is the Lord's Prayer in your Bible?

[2]See the book, *If the Foundations Be Destroyed* by Chick Salliby, available from Chick Publications.

QUESTION

Isn't it good enough that the missing words are in my NIV footnotes?

ANSWER

It is never "good enough" to take out or replace God's words. The text of the Bible is what the translators want you to think is the word of God. By putting the words into the footnotes, they make the reader think 1) they did not really belong in the Bible and 2) they are not really important.

But those words are **very** important (See the Bible verse comparisons on the next two pages).

There are many other examples. Many can be found in the excellent book, *If the Foundations Be Destroyed* by Chick Salliby. But these show us that every word of the Bible is very important. That is why God warns us about adding to or taking away from His words[1].

God's preserved words in the King James Bible are what we need as Christians, to prepare in this life for the life to come, and to know what God wants us to know. Anything short of that — is not God's word.

Footnotes:

[1]See Appendix C, "Are the Scriptures the "ideas" of God, or are they the words of God? *You* decide!"

Ephesians 4:6

KJV	NIV
One God and Father of all, who is above all, and through all, and in **you** all	one God and Father of all, who is over all and through all and <u>in all</u>

With an NIV it is pretty easy for a Christian Scientist to say that God is "in everyone," even those who have not accepted Jesus Christ as their Lord and Saviour.

Luke 2:33

KJV	NIV
And **Joseph** and his mother marveled...	The **child's father** and mother marveled...

Anyone who believed that Joseph, not God, was Jesus' true father would love the NIV (or any other of the Alexandrian perversions).

Mark 10:24

KJV	NIV
...Jesus answereth again... Children, how hard is it **for them that trust in riches** to enter into the kingdom of God!	...Jesus said again, "Children, <u>how hard it is to enter the kingdom of God!</u>"

The perversions spread the lie that it is hard to get to heaven. That makes it easy to say we need to do good works to be saved.

Mark 15:28

KJV	NIV
And the scripture was fulfilled, which saith, And he was numbered with the transgressors.	[Omitted]

This is the **only** place in the New Testament that shows us the fulfillment of this prophecy in Isaiah 53:12. The perversions hide a fulfilled prophecy!

Luke 9:54-56

KJV	NIV
54 ...Lord, wilt thou that we command fire to come down from heaven, and consume them, **even as Elias did?** **55** But he turned, and rebuked them, **and said, Ye know not what manner of spirit ye are of.** **56** **For the Son of man is not come to destroy men's lives, but to save them.** And they went to another village.	**54** ..."Lord, do you want us to call fire down from heaven to destroy them?" **[comparison with Elias omitted]** **55** But Jesus turned and rebuked them, **[Jesus' words of rebuke omitted]** **56** [Jesus' reason for coming to earth omitted] and they went to another village.

The NIV is meaningless! The true Bible shows that disciples are not to take revenge — "destroy lives" — but to "save them." The perversions **remove** the whole lesson.

QUESTION

Is anything missing from the New American Bible or the Rheims-Douay?

ANSWER

Actually, there are many words both added to and missing from these and all Roman Catholic Bibles.

Adding to Scripture

The New American, Douay/Rheims and other Roman Catholic Bibles add to Scripture.

Old Testament Apocrypha

The Roman Catholic Old Testament adds uninspired books, which we call Apocrypha, to the Bible, as if it were scripture.

- The additions to Esther
- Song of the Three Young Children
- Bel and the Dragon
- Judith
- Tobit
- Wisdom of Solomon
- Wisdom of Jesus ben Sirach
- I & II Maccabees

Roman Catholic Bibles, from the 300s AD to the present, include these uninspired Alexandrian Egyptian additions to Scripture. It wasn't until 1548 at the Roman Catholic Council of Trent that the Apocrypha was declared to be actual Scripture, in reaction to the Protestant Bibles. Translators of the King James Bible were told to include the Apocrypha. But they wrote seven excellent reasons why not to include it in Scripture. Alexander McClure, in his book *Translators Revived*[1] lists them:

1. Not one of them is in the Hebrew language, which was alone used by the inspired historians and poets of the Old Testament.

2. Not one of the writers lays any claim to inspiration.

3. These books were never acknowledged as sacred Scriptures by the Jewish Church, and therefore were never sanctioned by our Lord.

4. They were not allowed a place among the sacred books, during the first four centuries of the Christian Church.

5. They contain fabulous statements, and statements which contradict not only the canonical Scriptures, but themselves; as when, in the two Books of Maccabees, Antiochus Epiphanes is made to die three different deaths in as many different places.

6. It inculcates doctrines at variance with the Bible, such as prayers for the dead and sinless perfection.

7. It teaches immoral practices, such as lying, suicide, assassination and magical incantation.

The KJV translators were careful to **separate the Apocrypha from the Bible**, putting it in a separate section between the Old and New Testaments, with each page clearly labeled, "Apocrypha." The last page of II Maccabees, in the 1611 King James reads, "End of Apocrypha." Then it returns to God's inspired words in Matthew.

Taking Away From Scripture
New Testament
The Roman Catholic Bible is a perverted Alexandrian Egyptian Bible, not a preserved Antiochian Bible, like the King James. It is a combination of the heretical Egyptian Bible, including the Alexandrian Apocrypha, and blended to **look like** the preserved Vaudois Latin scriptures. It

omits thousands of words and a number of entire verses.

The Roman Catholic New American Bible (also called the "St. Joseph's Bible" is very similar, almost identical in New Testament text to many Protestant Bibles:

- NIV (1973, 1978) and TNIV (the 2002 "Gender-Neutral" revision of the NIV)
- English Revised Version (1881,1885) and its USA revision, American Standard (1901)
- Revised Standard (1946, 1952) and NRSV (its 1989 "Gender-Neutral" revision of the RSV)
- Revisions of the American Standard, such as the New American Standard (1962) and the Living Bible (1971)
- Today's English Version
- New English and Revised English Bibles
- Moffatt, Goodspeed, Wuest, J.B. Phillips and many other Protestant Bibles.

What's the Difference?

There is a lot added to and taken away from the Catholic Bibles. Most modern Protestant Bibles do not contain the Apocrypha like Catholic Bibles do. But there is almost **no difference at all** between the Roman Catholic New Testament and the modern Protestant perversions. Whichever you choose, ultimately you're being led down the primrose path of perversion. The only way to completely avoid this "broad way" is to take the narrow path and read the King James Bible.

Footnotes:
[1] Alexander McClure, *Translators Revived*, researched for 20 years and written in 1855 (See Appendix D).

Different Words

QUESTION

Don't Bibles with different words still say the same thing?

ANSWER

"Different words" produce different meanings. A "meaning that's different" from the truth is a lie. So if your Bible isn't a King James, it's lying to you about what God really said!

A Clear Case

For example, look at 1 Corinthians 7:36. The **King James Bible** accurately translates this passage:

> But if any man think that he behaveth himself uncomely toward **his virgin**, if she pass the flower of her age, and need so require, let him do what he will, he sinneth not: let them marry.

If a man has a virgin daughter (note that it says "**his** virgin," not "his betrothed") who is getting older, and "need so require," this father can allow them (the virgin and the man betrothed to her) to get married. Reading the scripture literally brings the clear solution, without pretending to find something "new" in the Greek. It's clear in the English! But now look at the NIV:

> If anyone thinks he is acting improperly toward the **virgin he is engaged to**, and <u>if she is getting along in years</u> and *he feels he ought to marry*, he should do as he wants. He is not sinning. They should get married.

NIV translators pretend the verse concerns, not the virgin's father, but the man she's engaged to! That's totally different! And it is wrong. Then the NIV wrongly changes "**need so *require***" to "**he *feels* he ought to**," putting the decision to marry, not up to "need," but the man's **feelings**! The new English Standard Version (ESV) and Revised Standard (RSV) take the lie a step further:

> If any one thinks that he is not behaving properly toward **his betrothed**, <u>if his passions are strong</u>, and *it has to be*, let him do as he wishes: let them marry— it is no sin.

Now the translators lied, saying the text is no longer considering *her* **passing youth**, but *his* **passions**!

The New English Bible is more ridiculous still:

> But if a man has **a partner in celibacy**c and <u>feels that he is not behaving properly towards her, if, that is, his instincts are too strong for him</u>d, and *something must be done*, he may do as he pleases; there is nothing wrong with it; let them marrye.
>
> c*Or* a virgin daughter   d*Or* if he is ripe for marriage   e*Or* let the girl and her lover marry

Now we have a multiple-choice Bible verse! They've completely changed the meaning. Again it talks about his *feelings*. But did you notice the next lie? If "**his instincts** are too strong for him"! This reflects the lie of evolution, saying man is like an animal with uncontrollable "instincts." This is a *lie*. God breathed into man, making him "a living soul" (Genesis 2:7). So humans have a soul and spirit, and they bear responsibility to follow God. No one can say "The devil made me do it," or "My instincts made me do it." When someone chooses evil, he or she will bear responsibility for it before the holy and righteous God (the Son), the Lord Jesus Christ.

Here you have blatant examples of a clear principle. When you change the **words** in a Bible passage so they no longer match the King James Bible, you end up changing the **meaning** of the passage.

The King James Bible was translated by over 50 Christians[1] who were experts in God's word and in many languages. Every single verse was considered **over fourteen times**[2]. No one got away with a new interpretation. **Every word of every verse had to pass the test of every other translator.** So the King James accurately translates God's preserved words from Greek and Hebrew into English. Modern so-called "scholars" like to translate what they *feel* the text says or what they *want* the text to say.

The Bottom Line

What kind of Bible do you want? Do you want to trust some "scholars" to give you what **they feel** the Bible *should* say? Or do you want to have a Bible that accurately translates the Greek and Hebrew so you can **know** what God *actually said*? I trust God the Holy Spirit to teach me the meaning of His words. I am seeking God's truth, not man's opinion. ***Which do you choose?***

Footnotes:
1 See page 21, "Who were the translators of the King James Bible?"
2 See page 28, "What method was used to translate the King James Bible?"

QUESTION

Can you prove the perverted Sinaiticus was found in a wastebasket?

ANSWER

Yes, I can. The Sinaiticus codex (Bible in book form) was deposited with lots of other paper, in the desire to burn it and bring warmth to the monastery. This story comes from many sources, including someone who knew the facts and examined the evidence for himself, and Tischendorf, the man who acquired the Sinaiticus.

There are many sources for the Sinaiticus story, that it was found after being deposited in a kindling bin at St. Catherine's monastery. Please remember: it gets COLD in monasteries! They needed to burn whatever they had to make themselves warm.

First I will tell you the story. I will go into detail about "who says what" regarding the finding of the Sinaiticus. Then I will present the conclusion.

The Story

This story is told by many people. The following are various scholars who recite this incident and about what happened to the texts:

I. John William Burgon (latter 1800s)

A contemporary of Constantin Tischendorf, himself an excellent Bible scholar, wrote *The Revision Revised* in 1883, after the English Revised New Testament and its perverted Greek text were released in 1881. **He is one of the only people ever to examine the Sinaiticus and Vaticanus, at length, for himself**. It is no coincidence, as a defender of the Received Text, that he was not invited to join the Revision Committee in 1871-1881. In his *The Revision Revised* [p. 319], Burgon stated:

> "We suspect that these two manuscripts are indebted for their preservation, 'solely to their ascertained evil character'; which has occasioned that the one eventually found its way, four centuries ago, to a forgotten shelf in the Vatican Library; while the other, after exercising the ingenuity of several generations of critical Correctors, **eventually** (viz in A. D. 1844) **got deposited in the wastepaper basket of the Convent at the foot of Mount Sinai.**" [emphasis mine]

> "Had B [Vaticanus] and ALEPH [Sinaiticus] been copies of average purity, they must long ago since have shared the inevitable fate of books which are freely used and highly prized; namely, they would have fallen into decadence and disappeared from sight."

Again, on pages 342-343, he said, tongue-in-cheek:

> "And thus it would appear that the Truth of Scripture has run a very narrow risk of being lost forever to mankind. Dr. Hort contends that it... lay 'perdu' (abandoned) on a forgotten shelf in the Vatican library;

> "Dr. Tischendorf [contends] **that it had been deposited in a wastepaper basket in the convent of St. Catherine** at the foot of Mount Sinai;— **from which he rescued it** on the 4th of February, 1859;

"—neither, we venture to think, a very likely circumstance. We incline to believe that the Author of Scripture hath not by any means shown Himself so unmindful of the safety of the Deposit, as these distinguished gentlemen imagine."

II. Dr. Benjamin G. Wilkinson (early 1900s)

In 1930, Benjamin Wilkinson published *Our Authorized Bible Vindicated* in England and America. In it he documents both the Preserved and Perverted manuscripts. Here is what he said about Tischendorf's discovery:

"The story of the finding of the Sinaitic Manuscript by Tischendorf in a monastery at the foot of Mt. Sinai illustrates the history of some of these later manuscripts.

"Tischendorf was visiting this monastery in 1844 to look for these documents. **He discovered in a basket, over forty pages of a Greek manuscript of the Bible. He was told that two other basket loads had been used for kindling.**

"Later, in 1859, he again visited this monastery to search for other manuscripts. He was about to give up in despair and depart when **he was told of a bundle of additional leaves of a Greek manuscript.** When he examined the contents of this bundle, he saw them to be a reproduction of part of the Bible in Greek. He could not sleep that night. Great was the joy of those who were agitating for a revision of the Bible when they learned that the new find was similar to the Vaticanus, but differed greatly from the King James."

(As quoted in David Otis Fuller, *Which Bible?*, p. 254, emphasis mine).

III. Norman L. Geisler and William E. Nix

Geisler and Nix (Later 1900s) in 1968 published (through the Moody Bible Institute of Chicago) the definitive work for Fundamentalists on the manuscripts of the Bible.

Because of their book, *A General Introduction to the Bible*, some of the most conservative of Christians in their Bible colleges finally abandoned the King James Bible and the *Textus Receptus*, and embraced the perverted 44 Alexandrian manuscripts as containing "something closer" to the long-lost truths of Scripture.

This book was used to raise the reputation of Westcott and Hort, and at every corner to denigrate the Byzantine texts, the Gothic and other preserved manuscripts (now represented in the *Textus Receptus*), and ultimately to try to sound a death-knell to the preserved words in the King James Bible.

Here is their section on the "Codex Sinaiticus (Aleph)", pp. 273-274, paragraphed and slightly edited for clarity [My comments appear in brackets]:

> "This fourth century Greek manuscript is generally considered to be the most important witness to the text because of its antiquity, accuracy[1], and lack of omissions.

> "The story of the discovery of aleph is one of the most fascinating and romantic in textual history.

> "It was found in the monastery of St. Catherine at Mount Sinai by the German Count Tischendorf, who was living in Prussia by permission of the czar.

"On his first visit (1844), he discovered **forty-three leaves of vellum, containing portions of the LXX (I Chronicles, Jeremiah, Nehemiah and Esther), in a basket of scraps which the monks were using to light their fires**. He secured it and took it to the University Library at Leipzig, Germany. It remains there, known as the Codex Frederico-Augustanus [*after his patron, Frederick Augustus, King of Saxony*].

"Tischendorf's second visit, in 1853, proved unfruitful; but in 1859, under the authority of Czar Alexander II, he returned again. Just before he was to return home empty-handed, **the monastery steward showed him an almost complete copy of the Scriptures and some other books**. These were subsequently acquired as a 'conditional gift' to the czar[2].

"This manuscript is now known as the famous Codex Sinaiticus (Aleph). It contains over half the Old Testament (LXX), and all of the New, with the exception of Mark 16:9-20 and John 7:53-8:11. All of the Old Testament Apocrypha, with the addition of the "Epistle of Barnabus", and a large portion of the "Shepherd of Hermas" are also included....

"In 1933 the British government purchased Aleph for the British Museum for 100,000 pounds, about $500,000 at that time. It was published in a volume entitled 'Scribes and Correctors of Codex Sinaiticus' (London, 1938)...." [emphasis mine]

IV. Constantin von Tischendorf

Here is the testimony of Tischendorf himself (1844):

"I perceived **in the middle of the great hall a large and wide basket, full of old parchments; and the librarian informed me that two heaps of papers like this, mouldered by reason of age, had been already committed to the flames.** What was my surprise **to find among this heap of documents a considerable number of sheets of a copy of the Old Testament in Greek**, which seemed to me to be one of the most ancient I had ever seen."

The following comes from *Which Version: Authorized or Revised?* by Philip Mauro (around the 1920s), as printed in *True or False?* by David Otis Fuller (1973, p. 71):

"The monks allowed him to take forty-five of the sheets. But nothing more transpired until fifteen years later, when he again visited the monastery, this time under the direct patronage of the Czar of Russia. **And then he was shown a bulky roll of parchment leaves, which included,** among other manuscripts of lesser importance, **the Codex now known as the Sinaitic**.

"Naturally enough Dr. Tischendorf was highly elated by his discovery. Indeed his enthusiasm was unbounded. He says,

"'I knew that I held in my hands the most precious Biblical treasure in existence;' and he considered this discovery to be 'greater than that of the Koh-i-noor (diamond) of the Queen of England.'"

V. Dr. Samuel C. Gipp, in *The Answer Book*, (1996 printing), had this to say:

> "One of the most prominent manuscripts which has been discovered since 1611 is the Sinaitic manuscript. **This witness, though horribly flawed, was found amongst trash paper in St. Catherine's monastery** at the foot of Mt. Sinai in 1841 by Constantine Tischendorf." (p. 110)

VI. Dr. Thomas Holland

Thomas Holland, a man for whom I have great respect, has discussed these and other issues in his online King James Bible Preservation Lessons, which now can be found in his book *Crowned With Glory: The Bible from Ancient Text to Authorized Version*. He agrees completely with Philip Mauro and Tischendorf[3].

VII. James R. White

James White is no friend to those who believe God preserved His words, or that the King James Bible is the English representative of that preservation. In his scathing book, *The King James Only Controversy: Can You Trust the Modern Translations?* (Minneapolis, Minnesota: Bethany House Publishers, 1995), White vilifies the King James camp, making unsupported statements and sweeping generalizations of the kind of people that believe the King James is God's preserved words. He gives an account of Tischendorf's search for manuscripts at St. Catherine's:

> "The single greatest example of an uncial codex written on vellum is Codex Sinaiticus, which today is almost always abbreviated with the single symbol of the Hebrew letter 'aleph,'... This great codex

contains the vast majority of the Bible, both Old and New Testaments, in Greek. The story of how it was found is evidence of God's providence.[4]

"Constantin von Tischendorf embarked on a journey to the Middle East in 1844 searching for biblical manuscripts. While visiting the monastery of St. Catherine on Mount Sinai, **he noted some scraps of parchment in a basket that was due to be used to stoke the fires in the oven of the monastery**. Upon looking at the scraps he discovered that they contained part of the Septuagint[5], the Greek translation of the Old Testament.

"This was exactly what he was looking for, and so **he asked if he could take the scraps to his room for examination, warning the monks that they should not be burning such items**. His obvious excitement worried the monks, who became less than cooperative in providing further information about manuscripts at the monastery.

"Years passed by. Tischendorf attempted to find more manuscripts at the monastery in 1853 but to no avail.

"Six years later he visited yet once again, and this time on the very evening before he was to leave he presented a copy of the Septuagint (which he had published) to the steward. Upon looking at Tischendorf's gift, **the steward remarked that he, too, had a copy of the Septuagint. From the closet in his cell he produced a manuscript, wrapped in a red cloth.** The monk had no idea of the treasure he held in his hands, for **this was none**

other than the Codex Sinaiticus, which at that time was no less than 1,500 years old!

"Tischendorf, having learned his lesson years earlier, hid his amazement and asked to examine the work. He spent all night poring over it, and attempted to purchase it in the morning, but was refused. The story of how the codex was eventually obtained is long, involved, and controversial. It resides today in the British Museum." (pp. 32-33) [emphasis mine].

A Helpful Summation

Here is a simple timeline, utilizing the above data, to make the story understandable.

1844 – Tischendorf goes to St. Catherine's monastery, at the foot of what is called "Mt. Sinai." He finds a pile/can of trash/kindling to be burned (Monasteries get very cold!) It has a bundle of manuscript sheets in it. He is told two other piles like it were already kindling. He gets permission for 43 sheets only. His enthusiasm makes him suspect to the monks. They tell him about no more "kindling" (manuscripts).

The 43 sheets are taken to the University Library at Leipzig, Germany. They are known as the Codex Frederico-Augustanus.

1853 – Tischendorf returns to St. Catherine's Monastery. He finds no more manuscripts anywhere, and no one shows him any.

1859 – Tischendorf's third trip to the monastery, this time under the authority of Czar Alexander II. On February 4th, the last day of his visit, he gives one of his published "Septuagint" books to the steward. The steward in turn shows Tischendorf a copy he held back: A codex, not in the trash (at least now), wrapped in red cloth. Tischendorf pores over it that night.

He attempts to buy the "Sinaiticus" (as we now call it) and is rebuffed. He tells them that the czar would be on their side if they made it a gift.

November: They accept, as a "conditional gift." Silver and rubles were paid to some monasteries, and the leaders were conferred Russian decorations.

1933 – The British government buys Sinaiticus for 100,000 pounds and it is placed in the British Museum.

1938 – The text is published (note: it is not photographed to show what the text actually looks like) in "Scribes and Correctors of Codex Sinaiticus" at London.

Fodder for Kindling

Here is where the trash bin/kindling bin comes in: Tischendorf does not say that the codex Sinaiticus was in the trash/kindling bin. But John Burgon does. And he was THERE: He actually saw the manuscripts and pored over them (both the Sinaiticus and Vaticanus, plus scores of others around Europe during his journeys). He must have spoken to the monks in the monastery. He knew Tischendorf. He was a factual person, leaning on evidence for just about every thing he has written.

The most likely scenario is that Burgon was right: The Sinaiticus WAS originally in the piles of paper to be burned. But just like my children, who only want one of their toys when "someone else" wants it, so the monks at St. Catherine's (or at least the steward) thought twice afterward about whether they would burn the ancient codex or keep it, much less ever give it away. So the huge codex was rescued, now realizing its value, and kept it in a private place, wrapping it in a red cloth to set it apart from the kindling.

The question is: will you place your faith in fireplace kindling, or the preserved words of the living God?

Footnotes:

[1]The Sinaiticus was not "accurate." When examining the text, we can see the truth. For 7 centuries after it was written, 10 different correctors tried to make it more like the preserved Bible, but finally gave up. So which one of the 11 different writers was supposed to be "accurate"?

[2]The footnote gives more details. "Actually, Tischendorf pulled a bit of 'ecclesiastical diplomacy' in convincing the monastery that it would be to their advantage for them to give the manuscript to the czar, whose influence as protectorate of the Greek Church could be to their advantage. In return for the manuscript, the czar gave them a silver shrine, 7,000 rubles for the library at Sinai, 2,000 rubles for the monks in Cairo, and conferred several Russian decorations on the authorities of the monastery."

[3]Note Lesson 4, "Early Heresies and the Western and Alexandrian Line" in the online lessons and *Crowned with Glory*, Chapter 2, "Tampering with Texts." For more on this and his other writings, visit Dr. Holland's site: http://hometown.aol.com/Logos1611/index.html.

[4]For a fuller description of the story, the book recommends that the reader see Bruce Metzger's *The Text of the New Testament: Its Transmission, Corruption, and Restoration*, 2nd ed. (Oxford: 1968), pp. 42-45).

[5]See page 47, "What Is the Septuagint?"

Corrupt Manuscripts

QUESTION

Can I read the NIV and still be saved? Really, I don't
see where the NIV, NASV and NKJV pervert the
doctrines of the church Jesus began. Your arguments only
serve to divide Christians by placing doubt where none
should be. I came to Christ through a Chick Tract when I
was 12, and believe it is an essential ministry. Everything
about your organization and what you are doing for the
Kingdom of God is admirable, but this continued bashing
of those who are not KJV believers only tends to ruin
what you are doing in the first place. I challenge you to
show me that I am lost and am going to hell because I
read the NIV. You won't have a leg to stand on.

ANSWER

I know no person who gauges Christianity (salvation, I
mean) by which Bible he reads.

Salvation Only Based on One Thing

I too, as you, have a Chick tract to thank for my
salvation, as I do Almighty God. But when I got saved, I
was immediately turned to the NASV. I didn't lose my
salvation. Then I read the ASV 1901. I didn't lose my
salvation. Then I read the RSV, the NKJV, then the NIV,
then the NKJV again for another decade. I have been
saved over 21 years, and I guarantee you, I never lost my
salvation for reading another Bible, even when I spent
time reading the Roman Catholic New American Bible,
and the Jesuit-written Douay-Rheims, the latter because it

was SO SIMILAR to the United Bible Society's 3rd edition Greek Text.

Salvation is based on the shed blood of our precious Lord and Saviour, God the Son and Son of God, Jesus Christ, and faith in His atoning death. It is NEVER based upon a preference of book reading!

If anyone has said that, then almost all of us at Chick Publications would be going to hell, for having read the "other" Bibles.

All Bibles Are NOT OK

That said, I cannot say that "all Bibles are OK." Have you read the Jehovah's Witnesses' Bible? One day I read to my church a number of verses. I asked them if they sounded right. None agreed. They all agreed that something was wrong. Then I showed them the camouflaged Bible I read from was a JW's New World Translation. Everyone was relieved. Then I told them: "Every verse you heard is essentially the same in the NIV." Mouths were stopped. People gasped. It was a great effect! I had made a point.

But I'm not some died-in-the-wool, ignorant, raised-in-a FundaMENTAList-church-and-never-grown-beyond-my-instilled-doctrines-type Christian, either.

My Education

I got my Bachelors of Arts at what is now called Hope University, Fullerton, California, in Linguistics and Bible. I got my Masters of Divinity degree at Fuller Theological Seminary, Pasadena, California, in General Theology, majoring in Linguistics. I took the three year Summer Institute of Linguistics courses with Wycliffe Bible Translators. I was top Greek student in Bible college and

walked into Advanced Greek in seminary, thrilling my
ASV/NIV/NASV using denomination. After that, I spent
years as a curious post-graduate, buying books about the
co-called Majority Text (Hodges/Farstad), the newer
Nestles/UBS Greek texts, buying copies of ancient
versions, etc. No one who has known me the last two
decades can deny that. I am far from an ignoramus on
these issues, to be blunt.

My Challenge

When one (count them: ONE) of my friends brought up
the issue of the King James (he's a full-grown father,
grandfather, college-educated, etc.), I really disagreed, but
he prayed for me anyway! He would bring up a small
thought, a seminal idea, and I would (as is my nature) go
crazy looking up references, versions, Greek, Hebrew,
linguistics and history. (Funny I'm so big on history now:
I got a C in History years ago. I guess I wanted to find out
the truth, and I just got better at it.) Gradually he started
making points with me.

I spent years researching the Roman Catholic religion,
simultaneously to the Bible history and version issue. A
few years ago, the research began to dovetail: Roman
Catholic names were found involved with what happened
to change the Protestant Bible into a Jesuit Roman
Catholic Bible.

Two Histories

See, there are two histories, not just one, that emerged.
If you don't mind my being simplistic, let me describe
them:

Apostolic	Apostate (disbelieved cardinal doctrines-heretics)
Antioch (Acts 11:26)	Alexandria, Egypt (never a good thing said about it)
Preserved words of God	Perverted words of God
5,322 manuscripts: massively agree.	44 manuscripts. No two consecutive verses agree!
Persecuted, Bibles burned and their people killed	Persecutors, killed Christians and burned their Bibles
Manuscripts Reformed the Christians	Manuscripts Deformed the Roman Catholic "Church."
Bibles without Apocrypha	Apocrypha COMES from Alexandrian "Bibles"!
Bibles lead to Tyndale to Rogers to Coverdale, to Great Bible to Geneva, to Bishop's Bible to the King James Bible.	Bibles lead to Constantine's "Bibles," to RC Latin Vulgate to Jesuit 1582/1610 Rheims/Douay to its 1850s revision to the New American Bible (all Roman Catholic); Protestant Side: Revised Version (1881), made with the SAME MANUSCRIPTS, and all those that followed, such as the NIV, ASV, RSV, TEV, NASV, NRSV, NEB, REB, Good News, New Living, and almost 200 others!

The King James version brought revival.	The "per-versions" brought a revival — of doubt.
The King James version brought the missionary movement.	The Catholic versions caused people to submit to Rome.
The KJV helped found the USA.	The Catholic versions helped keep people in spiritual bondage.
The KJV helped people say: "Thus saith the LORD!"	The modern Alexandrian versions quenched God's words. People said, "thus saith my teacher!"

Reluctant to Switch

I could go on. Do you see a difference? I didn't want to go to the King James Bible. My prejudices against it were so high that I said people could ONLY read it if the only other option was the Living Bible! I bought people NIVs by the dozens (literally), but never recommended the KJV.

When I found these and many more facts, backing up the definitive, normative, actual text being the Antiochian, Vaudois, Reformation, King James line, I didn't want to switch! But I was convicted by the evidence. I'd get old history books and check the timeline. Guess what? I found Gail Riplinger told the truth! And when I read her *New Age Bible Versions*[1] book, I remembered my own occult upbringing. She's no liar. But I realized: Someone WAS lying!

Who's the Liar?

There are only two possibilities here. There are only two arguments. There are only two sides. One side says the Alexandrian texts are the best we can get. The other side says the Antiochian texts are God's preserved words. Let's take a look at the argument and the associated evidence for each.

The Alexandrian Side

On one side is the concept that the "scholars in Alexandria, Egypt" produced a near-perfect, near original text. The problem is that of four manuscripts, each a huge, expensive, elaborately made codex (book), a man who spent a massive amount of time could find **no two consecutive verses that were the same!** So there is no consistent witness at all. They all disagree, both with each other and the Antiochian side. And the people in Alexandria didn't believe that Jesus was eternally God, that the Holy Ghost was eternally God, or that the miracles of the Old Testament actually happened. They were said to "spiritualize" the scriptures. They merged Greek Philosophy with Biblical texts. Such is the Alexandrian side. That represents both the Roman Catholics and Greek Orthodox, and the Protestants who use "new versions." After the Roman Catholic Latin Vulgate was made, largely using the Alexandrian manuscripts, but forming it like the Old Latin Vulgate, they spent 900 years killing anyone who had the Old Latin Vulgate.

The Antiochian Side

On the other side is the concept that the city where Paul and Barnabus taught, where "the disciples were called Christians first" (Acts 11:26) is the city where scriptures were preserved. The Antiochians were said to be "hyper-literal." If I had to choose someone to preserve God's words, it would be a hyper-literalist! From there, in 120

AD, the apostolic groups reached the Vaudois, a group of people in the Piedmont French valley of the Alps. These people were isolated, and after releasing their translation of the scriptures in their Old Latin in 157 AD, it became the Common Bible, or "Vulgate." This is the book the Roman Catholics tried to duplicate in form, but mostly using the Alexandrian manuscripts.

Which would you choose, if you had to choose? The Alexandrian side is clearly Roman Catholic. The Apocrypha comes from the same "codices" as the so-called "Septuagint" and the Alexandrian New Testament, which I afore mentioned. My choice is clear. I choose the preserved over the perverted, the Apostolic over the apostate, the Antiochian over the Alexandrian, "Thus saith the LORD" over "Thus saith my teacher."

Please examine the evidence. I do not condemn you. If you are saved, you are my brother. And like a brother, I urge you to consider these things.

Footnotes:
[1]See the review of her book in Appendix D.

QUESTION

Is the Lamsa Bible trustworthy like the King James Bible?

ANSWER

I used the Lamsa Bible when I was into the occult, over two decades ago. But I still remember the strange things it says to this day. The Lamsa Bible is supposedly a translation of the Aramaic Peshitta Bible, authored by occultist George Lamsa. He was a very sly man. He used as his base text the King James Bible, and changed passages to fit what he wanted them to say, then claimed he was only "translating the Aramaic."

Perverted Prophecies of the Lord Jesus Christ

For example, in Matthew 27:46 God's words say:

"And about the ninth hour Jesus cried with a loud voice, saying, Eli, Eli, lama sabachthani? that is to say, My God, my God, **why hast thou forsaken me?**"

But Lamsa's book says "Eli, Eli, lemana shabakthani," which according to his notes means, "My God, my God, **for this I was spared**," or "**this was my destiny**." This destroys the Lord Jesus Christ's quotation of Psalm 22:1. Even worse, he changed Psalm 22:1 into heresy:

My God, my God, why hast thou **let me to live**? and yet thou hast *delayed my salvation from me*, because of the words of my folly.

A person reading Jesus' words on the cross and Psalm 22 would have **no idea** that God made that psalm into a precise prophecy of the crucifixion of the Lord Jesus Christ.

We know that the Lord Jesus is the "**only-begotten**" of

God the Father. But in Lamsa's perversion it reads, "the **first-born**" (John 1:14, 18). Jesus wasn't the *first* born from God; He is the **ONLY** one, God the Son and Son of God.

1 Timothy 3:16 says clearly "**God** was manifest in the flesh;" but Lamsa wrongly wrote, "**it** [the "divine mystery"] is revealed in the flesh." Jesus wasn't a mystery with a body. He was, and is, God Himself.

Micah 5:2 tells us that the Lord Jesus has always lived; but instead of "whose goings forth **have been from of old, from everlasting,**" Lamsa lies, "whose goings forth have been **predicted from of old, from everlasting.**" This makes no sense. Jesus wasn't *predicted* from eternity; He has *existed* from eternity!

Other Prophecies

He changed other passages, too, such as one in Daniel 11:38, which many believe prophesies the antichrist. The KJV clearly says: "But in his estate shall he honour the **God of forces**: and a god whom his fathers knew not shall he honour with gold, and silver, and with precious stones, and pleasant things." But in the Lamsa Bible, it says this evil man will honor "the **mighty God**..."

Isaiah 14:12 tells us about the spirit *behind* the kings of the world, namely **Lucifer**: "How art thou fallen from heaven, O Lucifer, son of the morning!" But in Lamsa's perversion it reads: "How are you fallen from heaven! **howl** in the morning!"

It's Not a Christian Bible

The Lamsa Bible is not Christian at all. It is Lamsa's own blend of occultic ideas made to look a lot like the King James Bible. Amazingly he published books with both Holman Publishers and the occultic Unity "School of Christianity." For a while, some Christians endorsed this Bible, and it was the choice for Oral Roberts' study Bible years back. I have not heard anything more about it for years.

It is better to stay with God's preserved words in English. All these supposed "more ancient" and "better" Bible texts have done is bring confusion to the Christian world. And we all know who is the author of confusion.

Other Languages

QUESTION
Has God only preserved a Bible for English-speaking people?

ANSWER
God has preserved His words through the broad flow of history in certain specific languages: Hebrew, Greek, Old Latin and English. Other languages have the blessed opportunity to follow what God has revealed and translate it into their languages.

People today say, "How dare you King James-only people! You just want to force people to translate the KJV into other languages!" But look at the NIV: That perversion is being translated all over the world, and it is STILL the NIV! The NVI in Spanish, for example, is not very different at all from the NIV. The Dutch, French and other versions are still NIVs! And the NIV is most definitely an English Bible.

So the question is not "Shall we translate the Bible from English into other languages?" The question is "Which Bible shall we use to translate God's words into the various languages of the world?" I know the King James Bible is God's preserved words in English. So my choice is made. May God help the translators of the world to use God's words, and not a perversion that will only bring them into judgment before our Almighty God.

QUESTION

Is the Spanish Bible, *La Biblia de las Americas*, corrupted like other modern Bible versions?

ANSWER

La Biblia de las Americas is simply the New American Standard in Spanish. It has the same Alexandrian perversions as the NASV, NIV, TEV, NCB, NEB, etc. It contains the error of "only begotten God" in John 1:18, and all the other errors of the New American Standard. It is not new, but has been around since the 1980s. However, the Lockman Foundation has been pushing it really hard in Spanish-speaking countries lately. They are trying to subvert the Reina-Valera as God's word to the Hispanic people.

No translation in Spanish is exactly like the King James. But the closest is the Reina-Valera. I use a Reina-Valera 1909. Many Spanish-speaking Christians, evangelists, and churches prefer the 1960, though it uses the Spanish form of the Greek Sheol and the Hebrew *Hades* instead of "hell" (*el infierno*) in various passages. In the 1960 version, the basic text behind the Reina-Valera is the *Textus Receptus*, but many words have been changed to follow modern perversions.[1]

If you want God's words as closely as possible in Spanish, I recommend the Reina-Valera, not any Spanish version of the NASV, NIV, Good News/Today's English Bible, or any other Alexandrian perversion.

Footnotes:

[1] For more on the differences in the 1960 and other Reina-Valera Bibles, see *The Elephant in the Living Room: Seeing the Shadow of the RSV in Spanish*, edited by Dr. Mickey P. Carter (Haines City, Florida: Landmark Baptist Press, 2002).

QUESTION
Are all Reina-Valeras the same?

ANSWER
I am not a Spanish scholar, so I cannot judge the translation of that language *per se*. But I do know a good Greek text from a bad one. Therefore this much I can tell you: All editions of the Reina-Valera are not alike! Some are very close to the KJV, while others are near-duplicates of the perverted Alexandrian bibles. Here is a simple history of good and bad editions of the Reina-Valera Spanish Bible. (The following information comes from the excellent review "The Spanish Fountain: A History and Review of the Reina-Valera Version,"[1] by Thomas Holland, Th. D., Author of *Crowned with Glory: The Bible from Ancient Text to Authorized Version*).

Casiodoro de Reina (1520-1594), a former Roman Catholic monk, published his translation of the Bible in 1569. It had a few problems. It omitted the words "by faith" in Romans 3:28, omitted all of Hebrews 12:29 ("For our God is a consuming fire") and included the Apocrypha.[2] One of his friends was Cipriano de Valera (1531-1602+), another former monk. In 1596 Valera published a revised translation of the New Testament, and in 1602 he finished the complete Bible in Spanish, following the *Textus Receptus* more than Reina had.

From 1622 through 1865 many people revised or reprinted the Reina-Valera Bible, changing words at times, (though not their meaning), and the Spanish people benefited from the best Spanish Bible they ever had.

But 243 years of peace were shattered when the American Bible Society (ABS) decided to radically change the Spanish Bible! Although they had not yet switched the preserved King James for the perverted "bible," they deceitfully changed the Spanish Bible into an Alexandrian perversion like the NIV or NASV, still calling it the Reina-Valera! The Bible in Spanish would never be the same.

From 1866 through 1899, a great tug-of-war ensued. During those years people printed the preserved line of Reina-Valera Bibles, as well as the ever-worsening ABS Alexandrian Bibles, all bearing the name "Reina-Valera." Finally in 1901, the Spanish-speaking people had had enough. From 1901-1909, the Christians revised the Reina-Valera back in line with the *Textus Receptus*. There were still a few differences between it and the King James. But for now, the preserved family of manuscripts had won.

From 1909 through 1959, the Spanish people again used this *Textus Receptus* Bible. In 1960 came a revision, again by the American Bible Society (ABS). Although changes were again made, making some parts more like the perversions, and some parts more like the KJV, it became the most popular Bible over the years. Another ABS revision occurred in 1978, again slightly changing the text.

But now in this new millennium the same threat has reared its ugly head. The two-year-old Sociedad Biblica Iberoamericana is preparing to release a new perversion: the Biblia Textual Reina-Valera. This new "Textual Bible" pretends to "fix" the *Textus Receptus*. Their solution? Change the Reina-Valera into the form of (are you ready for this?) the Westcott-Hort (Alexandrian) text! They promote Westcott, Hort, Eberhard Nestle (whose perverted Greek New Testament set the standard for today) and Bruce Metzger (who has backed the false Greek text and major translations like the Revised Standard and New Revised Standard). In other words, this Bible Society wants to palm off the same old devilish, Alexandrian manuscripts on an unsuspecting public.

Brothers and sisters, we have to be very careful about choosing which Bible to use. The preserved line of manuscripts in Spanish is used by the 1602, 1909 and 1960 Reina-Valeras, (although the 1960 clearly changes many verses to match the modern perversions). The Iberoamerican Bible Society's new "Biblia Textual Reina-Valera" or "Reina-Valera Textual Bible" is the same old Alexandrian trash delivered in fancy packaging. Choose your Bible carefully in any language. But in English, be thankful we have God's preserved words in English, the King James Bible.

Footnotes:

[1]"The Spanish Fountain: A History and Review of the Reina-Valera Version" by Thomas Holland is available to read online at a number of websites.

[2]The Apocrypha remained in the Reina-Valera until the "Santa Biblia" edition in 1862.

Chapter 6

What's Wrong with KJV Look-Alikes?

QUESTION

What is wrong with the New King James Version? All it does is modernize the words of the King James Bible, right? Why should I read the King James and not the helpful New King James?

ANSWER

The New King James is **not** a King James Bible. It changed thousands of words, ruined valuable verses, and when not agreeing with the King James Bible, it has instead **copied** the perverted NIV, NASV or RSV. And this you must know: those who translated the NKJV did **not** believe God perfectly preserved His words!

This question is very important to those who want God's truth in the English language. I myself used the NKJV for a decade before I learned the truth about God's preserved words. Here is some of what convinced me to switch to the King James Bible from the "New King James."

Changed Words Means Changed Meanings

We know that Bible versions disagree on how to translate certain words. Is Jesus God's "Son" or only God's "servant"?[1] If He is God's Son, then we all need to listen to what He said! Changed words like this make a great deal of difference in how we understand a passage.

Loss of "thee" and "thou"

Please decide what God is saying to Moses:

"And the LORD said to Moses, "How long do
you refuse to keep My commandments and My
laws?" (Exodus 16:28, NKJV)

It looks like God is saying, "Moses, you are continuing
to refuse to keep My commandments and My laws." But
look carefully at the accurate King James:

"And the LORD said unto Moses, How long refuse
ye to keep my commandments and my laws?"

Now we understand! God was upset with the **people**,
not Moses. In classical English "ye" and "you" mean
more than one person. "Thee," "thou," "thy," "thine,"
"doeth," "hast," etc., mean only **one** person. How do we
know? The "y" is plural. The "t" is singular. Isn't that
easy? Now you know what Jesus meant when He said to
Nicodemus, "Marvel not that I said unto thee, Ye must be
born again" (John 3:7).

What Jesus said was, "Nicodemus, marvel not that I said
unto thee, all of you need to be born again." This is very
important. Not only Nicodemus needed to be saved. But
everybody, including him, needed to be born again. That's
why Jesus used the plural.

But there is more of a problem than the thousands of
times "thee" and "thou" are removed from God's words.
What does a word mean? This is very important, as you
shall see.

Go to Gehenna?

The NKJV claims it is "more accurate" because it leaves
untranslated words like *Gehenna*, *Hades* and *Sheol*.
What do they mean? The King James gives you the **exact
meaning**: "hell." We know what that means. When's the
last time you heard someone say "Go to Gehenna"?

Which is correct?

The NKJV consistently uses terms that don't mean the same as the King James Bible. Here are some examples:

	King James Version	**New King James Version**
2 Corinthians 2:17	"For we are not as many which **corrupt** the word of God"	"**peddling** the word of God" [like the NIV, NASV and RSV]
Titus 3:10	"A man that is **an heretick** after the first and second admonition reject"	"Reject **a divisive man**" [like the NIV]
1 Thess. 5:22	"Abstain from **all appearance** of evil."	"Abstain from **every form** of evil." [like the NASV, RSV and ASV]
Isaiah 66:5	"...Your brethren that hated you, that cast you out for my name's sake, said, Let the LORD be glorified: but **he shall appear to your joy**, and they shall be ashamed." [This means that the LORD shall appear, which shall occur at the Second Coming of Christ.]	"...Your brethren who hated you, who cast you out for My name's sake, said, 'Let the LORD be glorified, **that we may see your joy.**' But they shall be ashamed." [Like the NIV, NASV, RSV and ASV, the Second Coming is wholly omitted from this scripture.]

Both translations cannot be correct. If one is right, the other has to be wrong. No matter how you slice it, the NKJV does not have the same meaning as the accurate King James Bible.

Changed Affections

There is a lot of evidence that the translators and publishers did not believe God preserved His words.

Thomas Nelson Publishers

The NKJV was translated and is printed under the watchful eye of Thomas Nelson Publishers. Here is part of a timeline they published.

1969

Sam Moore purchases Thomas Nelson Publishers, vowing to return it to its once proud place among the leading publishers of the world.

1976

Nelson initiates the creation of a new translation of the Bible –The New King James Version.

1980s

Nelson reclaims its place as a premier publisher of Bibles and Christian Books, expands into international markets, and establishes Markings® as Nelson's Gift division.

It is clear the NKJV made Thomas Nelson Publishers a lot of money. Did a King James-type Bible renew their hearts to God? Note the following facts:

• They are also the publishers of the American Standard Version, the American revision of Westcott and Hort's perverted English Revised Version.

- They are also the publishers of the Revised Standard Version, the revision of the American Standard.

- To this day they continue to sell at least six Bible perversions. The NKJV was just **one** moneymaker that helped Nelson "reclaim its place" as a major publisher.

- The NKJV repeats the lie that "There is only one basic New Testament used by Protestants, Roman Catholics, and Orthodox, by conservatives and liberals." In fact, there are two: the perverted Alexandrian line that was continued by the Roman Catholic religion and the preserved, apostolic, Antiochian line that progresses from the Christians at Antioch of Syria (Acts 11:26) to our precious King James Bible.

The New King James Translators

Marion H. Reynolds Jr. of the Fundamental Evangelistic Association reveals a little-known fact:

> The duplicity of the NKJV scholars is also a matter for concern. Although each scholar was asked to subscribe to a statement confirming his belief in the plenary, divine, verbal inspiration of the original autographs (none of which exist today), the question of whether or not they also believed in the divine preservation of the divinely inspired originals was not an issue as it should have been. Dr. Arthur Farstad, chairman of the NKJV Executive Review Committee which had the responsibility of final text approval, stated that this committee was about equally divided as to which was the **better** Greek New Testament text—the *Textus Receptus* or the Westcott-Hort. **Apparently**

none of them believed that either text was the Divinely preserved Word of God. Yet, all of them participated in a project to "protect and preserve the purity and accuracy" of the original KJV based on the TR. Is not this duplicity of the worst kind, coming from supposedly evangelical scholars?

Not "The Real Thing"

What Mr. Reynolds points out is very important. There were basically two groups of translators working on the NKJV. One half believed that the perverted 44 Alexandrian manuscripts, from which came the Roman Catholic Bibles and the modern perversions, were better than the manuscripts behind the King James. The other group believed the thousands of manuscripts supporting the King James were better. This is a big problem: No one believed that they held God's words in their hands, only a "better" or "worse" text! The translators believed they had something **close**, but **not an accurate Bible**. It is a sad thing when a Bible translator doesn't even believe he has God's words in his hands. It sounds like they don't believe God kept His promise:

> **Mark 13:31** Heaven and earth shall pass away: but my words shall not pass away.

Perhaps that is why some of them had no problem working on other perversions, both before and after working on the NKJV. This is so **unlike** the 54-plus Bible men who faithfully translated the King James Bible from preserved manuscripts of God's words. The difference between the King James and the "New" King James is the difference between day and night.

Compromising God's Words

Many Christians are discovering the miracle of God's words in English. But the enemy has tried to insert a monkey-wrench: the NKJV. Pastors approve it, "scholars" promote it, but the NKJV is a wolf in sheep's clothing. The New King James is just a **compromise** between the liberal, perverted Bible versions floating around and the rock-solid, accurate and preserved words of God, the King James Bible.

Brothers and sisters, don't settle for anything less than God's words.

Footnotes:

[1]In the modern perversions, including the NKJV, there are crucial passages in Acts 3 and 4 that change the correct word "son" for the unimportant word, "servant." All Christians are servants of God. But the Lord Jesus Christ is the only-begotten SON of God. (An article on this can be found online at:
http://www.chick.com/information/bibleversions/articles/saviororservant.asp.)

QUESTION
Do the King James and New King James use the same Hebrew and Greek?

ANSWER
The NKJV is **not** a revision of the King James Bible. The Greek and Hebrew behind the NKJV are the same as for the modern perversions. They are **not** the same as the Greek and Hebrew behind the King James Bible, God's preserved words in English.

A History of Preservation
There is a big difference between God's *preserved* words and man's *perverted* words.

Old Testament
God preserved the words of the Old Testament by the Levitical priests, who faithfully copied them through the centuries. The best manuscript, used by the King James Bible, was the Ben Chayyim, also called the "Bomberg Text." This faithful Rabbinic Old Testament, used for the King James Bible, was rejected by the NKJV committee in favor of a Vatican-published text.

New Testament
God preserved the words of the New Testament by His faithful Christian disciples, from Antioch of Syria (Acts 11:26) to the Vaudois people of the French Alps about AD 120. From the 150s on they passed this Old Latin Bible (called "Common Bible" or "Vulgate") throughout Europe and the British Isles. The Vaudois people were regarded by the Protestants and Baptists as "pre-Reformers," passing down the gospel message till the Reformation of the 1500s. Their Bibles and others translated from them,

were so accurate they were included in translating the King James Bible. The NKJV committee unwisely used none of these Bibles.

The Preserved vs. the Perverted "Vulgate"

Remember: the Vaudois' *Old Latin* Vulgate is not the same as the later *Roman Catholic* Latin Vulgate. The Vaudois' Vulgate is God's preserved words in Old Latin which brought the gospel to all Europe. The *Roman Catholic* Vulgate is completely different. It wrongly mixed God's words with the perverted Alexandrian Greek Old Testament, Apocrypha and New Testament. Modern "scholars" falsely declare there's only one Latin Vulgate. But there are *two*: the preserved (Vaudois) and the perverted (Roman Catholic).

A Mixture of Perversion

The New King James Version is **not** a true King James Bible. It mixes some true King James accuracy with a lot of Alexandrian and "new version" errors. We know this because the NKJV tells us **which** texts they used when they made up their Bible. Don't be fooled by the clever names and symbols. Here is what they *really* used:

• The Biblia Hebraica Stuttgartensia, or BHS. This is **not** the preserved Hebrew Old Testament. This one is approved by the **Vatican** (Roman Catholic religion) and printed jointly by the Vatican and Protestant Bible societies. In 1937 the "scholars" **rejected** the preserved Ben Chayyim for an "older" (but not more accurate) text: the Leningrad Ms B 19a (also called the "*Ben Asher* text"). The BHS states:

...it is a welcome sign of the times that it was published jointly in 1971 by the Wurttemburg Bible Society, Stuttgart, and the Pontifical Biblical Institute, Rome... (Prolegomena, p. XII)

- <u>The Septuagint, or LXX</u>. As you have seen[1], the so-called "Septuagint" is a fable. It was really written *after* Jesus was born, not before. There are *many* Septuagints, since each Alexandrian Old Testament is *different* from every other. Know what they are? Sinaiticus, Vaticanus and Alexandrinus—the same codices (big books) where the modern perverted **New Testaments** come from!

- <u>The Latin Vulgate.</u> This is **not** the preserved Vaudois Christian, Old Latin Vulgate. The NKJV "scholars" consulted the perverted, **Roman Catholic** Latin Vulgate.

- <u>The Dead Sea Scrolls, or DSS.</u> It is clear through Scripture that God preserved His words through the tribe of Levi (Deuteronomy 17:18, 31:9-13, 25-26, Nehemiah 8 and Malachi 2:7). The Qumran community that produced the DSS are **never** said to be Levites. But though God says "the **priest's** lips should keep knowledge, and they should seek the law at his mouth" (Malachi 2:7), the NKJV committee instead consulted the DSS as well.

- <u>The Majority Text, or MT.</u> With a name like **Majority Text** it *should* be a compilation of the **majority** of Greek New Testament manuscripts. **But it is not.** The "Majority Text" is actually a hand-picked set of manuscripts grouped together by "pro-Alexandrian" liberal Hermann von Soden. Less than **8%** of the over 5,000 Greek manuscripts were compared to each other by von Soden!

But the NKJV people give the MT great prominence, writing this inaccurate information in the footnotes. So people **think** that the King James is wrong, since it disagrees with "the Majority Text." Who cares? The "Majority Text" is **not** the majority of texts! The "Majority Text" is a **big fake**. Don't believe it. And don't trust any Bible that does.

If It Looks Like a Duck and Talks Like a Duck...

There is another side to the New King James that reveals its ugly alliances. Take a look at these examples:

Verse	King James Version	New King James Version	Perversions agreeing with NKJV
Acts 3:26	God, having raised up his **Son**	His **Servant**	NIV, NASV, ASV, RSV, Roman Catholic New American Bible (NAB), etc.
Acts 17:22	...in all things ye are **too superstitious**.	**very religious**	NIV, NASV, ASV, RSV, Roman Catholic NAB, etc.
Romans 1:25	Who **changed** the truth of God **into** a lie	who **exchanged** the truth of God **for** the lie	NIV, NASV, ASV, RSV, Roman Catholic NAB, etc.

1 Cor. 1:18	…but unto us which are **saved** it is the power of God.	…who are **being saved** [The Roman Catholic lie that salvation is a process.]	NIV, NASV, NASU (NASV Revision in 1995), RSV, Roman Catholic NAB, etc.

In most places where the NKJV disagrees with the King James Bible, it agrees with the Alexandrian perversions, whether Protestant like the NIV, NASV, RSV, ASV, etc., or Roman Catholic like the New American Bible.

The King James Bible is God's preserved words in English. The NKJV is just man's **most subtle perversion** of God's words. Don't be deceived. Insist on the King James Bible, not "New" King James, "Modern" King James, King James "2" or "21" or "Millennium." Even though it is very **similar** to a King James Bible, it is **not** a King James Bible. Insist on the one you can stake your faith on, the genuine King James Bible. God will bless you.

Footnotes:

[1]See page 47, "What is the Septuagint?"

QUESTION

Isn't the 21st Century King James an exact reprint of the original 1611 KJV, updating archaic words? Can I trust it? Why does the original 1611 version have "strain out a gnat" and modern King James versions misprint that by saying "strain at a gnat" When will this error be corrected?

ANSWER

The 21st Century King James Bible is not really a true King James Bible at all. I trust only what God has blessed. Do you have any evidence of massive revival sweeping the land with ANY modern version but the King James, from 1611 to the present? Of missionary movements inspired by those believing it? Of preachers who are SURE they are preaching "thus saith the Lord"? I don't trust any fake KJV. Just the real one.

You were lied to about Matthew 23:24. It is a lie spread by anti-King James people. It is important to be careful and not just believe every anti-King James accusation you read on the web. Many of them are simply incorrect. Check them out before you believe them!

I have a letter-for-letter exact reproduction (I know a couple who've spent thousands on research materials, and they checked every letter; this is an exact Bible I have) of the 1611 King James Bible, first printing by Robert Barker, the King's own printer. Here's exactly what it says:

> Ye blind guides, which straine at a gnat, and swallow a camel.

There you have it. The King James NEVER said "strain out a gnat." It ALWAYS said, in proper English, "strain at a gnat." The modern printings that say "strain at a gnat" are correct. Sure, NOW we say "strain out," but that's new. We're the ones who have changed. The Cambridge King James Bible is an exact replica, with updated spelling and all printing errors removed, of precisely what the translators handed Robert Barker to be printed![1]

In short, there is no error, thus nothing to be corrected, in accurate printings of the King James Bible like the Cambridge. I come from a totally anti-KJV training in Bible college and seminary. It has taken years of research to dispel the stories and lies and doubts placed on God's preserved words, the King James Bible.

Footnotes:
[1]See page 126, "Has the King James Bible been changed between 1611 and today?"

Chapter 7

What Will I Do?

QUESTION
What will You do when they know it's not true?

Once upon a time there was a missionary in a far-off land. He cared about the people there. He wanted them to know the gospel. So he began translating the Bible into their language the way he had been taught.

But when he came to Luke 15 he faced a problem. "These people don't know what a sheep is," he said. "They have never seen one. How do I teach them the parable of the lost sheep if they don't know what a sheep is?" Then he remembered his training. "I need to do one of two things. I could teach these people about "sheep" and make up a new word for it in their language. Or I could find a dynamic equivalent for sheep in their culture." He decided the second was easier. And so he found an animal the people cared for like a sheep: a guinea pig.

And so he translated the Bible, finding dynamic equivalents wherever he thought he needed to. "I don't need to teach these people all about Israel, the Hebrews and their culture," he thought. And finally he published this "Bible" and gave it to the people. They loved their Bible and read from it often. Some even became Christians and moved away to a school to learn more.

One day a student returned to his family and confronted

the missionary. "Why did you change the Bible?" he demanded. "The Bible doesn't have guinea pigs and jungles, you liar!" "But I thought you wouldn't understand," replied the missionary. "No! You told us lies about what God said! How can we ever trust you again?" So the people no longer believed the missionary. All his work was ruined and he went home in disgrace.

There are only two ways to bring the gospel to people. You can tell them God's words and help them to understand what they mean. Or you might change the truth to make it easy for them and hope they never find out. *But if you do, what will you do when they know it's not true?*

QUESTION

What should I do with my new version Bibles now that I know the KJV is correct? I don't want to give them away (the NKJV and NASV) as they are full of fallacies. Should they be destined for the trash?

ANSWER

You have a valuable resource in those perversions of God's word! As you find examples of errors, omissions and completely changed verses, you can mark them to show your friends. I will do all I can to provide lists and examples of where the other English versions fall flat.

I like to highlight the changes. For example, I have marked my Jehovah's Witness New World Translation with the proper readings of the King James Bible[1]. Then I can easily compare it to other perversions to show how the JW Bible is nearly identical to the NIV, NASV, RSV, etc.

Another kind of change to note (for your NKJV, for example) is where the New King James reads the same as a NASV, NIV, or RSV. Check Song of Solomon for a pile of word-for-word copying. If the NKJV were supposed to be an "updating" of the King James, why use the word changes from the modern perversions?

You can have great fun and quite a learning experience by noting and marking changes in modern perversions. If you find anything really interesting, please send it to me. It would be a pleasure to post more proof of the horrible mistake people make when they abandon God's words in English, the King James Bible.

---

[1] A great place to start finding changes in modern perversions is Chick Salliby's *If the Foundations Be Destroyed*, available from Chick Publications.

QUESTION

What about people who can't understand the King James? I know some people who basically refuse to read the KJV because they claim they don't understand it. However, they are willing to read the NIV. I feel bad recommending the NIV to them if they aren't willing to read the KJV because I do feel that the KJV is the word of God. But in a case like this, is it better to have them read the NIV over nothing at all?

ANSWER

A false Bible is not the truth. It's that simple. I am a kind and soft-hearted person. I would love to tell people it is okay to read other Bibles, and just as good for them. That's my personality. But I cannot compromise the truth and tell people that a Bible that is missing or adding to or changing the truth is STILL the truth. False Bibles are not "The Truth, The Whole Truth, and Nothing but the Truth."

I must tell people the truth. I learned it at 17 when I began reading a King James Bible and needed to understand it. This truth is simple: It is by the Holy Ghost that we understand the King James Bible. Look at these scriptures.

> **Luke 24:45** Then opened he their understanding, that they might understand the scriptures,

> **1 Corinthians 2:12-16** Now we have received, not the spirit of the world, but the spirit which is of God; that we might know the things that are freely given to us of God. Which things also we speak, not in the words which man's wisdom teacheth, but which the Holy Ghost teacheth; comparing spiritual things with spiritual. But the natural man receiveth not the things of the Spirit

of God: for they are foolishness unto him: neither can he know them, because they are spiritually discerned. But he that is spiritual judgeth all things, yet he himself is judged of no man. For who hath known the mind of the Lord, that he may instruct him? But we have the mind of Christ.

Acts 17:11 These were more noble than those in Thessalonica, in that they received the word with all readiness of mind, and searched the scriptures daily, whether those things were so.

It is by God's great grace that we can understand His words. Here is what I did. Just as the Bible says, I pray to the Father (Colossians 3:17; 1 Peter 1:17) in the name of Jesus, God the Son (Matthew 18:20; John 14:13-14; 15:16), and ask that the Holy Ghost reveal the scriptures to me (John 14:26; 15:26; 1 Corinthians 2:12-16).

Since the first day I prayed that way to God, even though I was still in the occult, the Lord began to show me His truth as I read His words in the King James Bible. Two weeks later I was saved!

What's more, I was amazed to find out two years later in Bible college that what God had shown me about the Bible was correct. What a blessing! And God is "no respecter of persons" (Acts 10:34) so what He did for me He will do for anyone who asks Him.

If we need help with words we do not understand, we use a Bible dictionary or the *King James Bible Companion*. But when we do not understand Bible teaching, we pray to our God, in Jesus' name, who by the Holy Ghost richly supplies "all things that pertain unto life and godliness" (2 Peter 1:3).

QUESTION

Why did you create the *King James Bible Companion*[1]?

ANSWER

When I became convicted that 1) God had promised to preserve His words and 2) that the King James Bible is God's preserved words in English, I noticed lists that supposedly had "archaic" words and their "correct meanings." As I read them, I knew that many were wrong. People assumed that the new Bible versions had correctly translated the words, and merely substituted the readings from the NASV, NIV and other perversions to "translate" the KJV vocabulary.

The truth was that these lists did not translate the King James words. So I wanted to make a new list that gave the correct meaning of KJV words. I searched books on etymology (history and meaning of words) and ancient dictionaries. Then I checked every place in the Bible where each word appeared, and made sure which meanings were correct in each Bible passage. Those definitions made it onto my list. In addition, I listed at least the first verse where each word appeared in the Bible with that specific definition.

Chick Publications decided to print the book, and it now has over 400,000 copies in print. May God bless you as you study and believe God's preserved words in English, the King James Bible.

Footnotes:

[1]The *King James Bible Companion is available* from Chick Publications. Or you may purchase it as part of the *SwordSearcher* Bible software at www.swordsearcher.com. Or download it for your PDA at www.handstory.com

Conclusion

The truth is out there, if we are willing to look. But many people don't spend the time to find it out. Pastors have their church programs to attend to. Teachers have their lessons to plan. Students simply believe their professors and forget to question what they are told. And the lie is passed on.

Why doesn't my pastor, teacher or professor know the truth? The answer is simple. They never questioned their teachers. They never examined the evidence.

God gave His words. God preserved His words. And His words are perfectly preserved in English in the King James Bible. That is what is proven in this book. The evidence is before you.

I pray God will give you the confidence to share this truth with your friends, your teachers, and of course, your pastor.

May God richly bless you as you do.

In Christ Jesus, and for His service,

David W. Daniels

Appendix A

Why Should I Believe You?

I've read your words concerning the differences between the Bible versions. **Question #1, Who are you?** Why should I place trust in you when I have seen so many "Christians" totally fleece others and destroy their faith?

Question #2, Why should I believe you? I have been a Christian for less than 3 years, so I won't pretend to know close to anything when it comes to the entirety of the Bible, but I have been blessed; I read the NKJV and NIV.

Question #3, Where did you get your information? I will not jump off a boat just because it is leaning on the waves. I will not jump away from the NIV because somebody says it lies. All my life I was told God was not real and the KJV was written to placate the king, not God. I need proof. You've got my attention; prove your words without trying to sell me something.

ANSWER

It is necessary to answer your questions one by one.

1. **Who am I?** I am a born-again Christian believer for over 20 years, who only cares about the truth. I got my bachelor's degree in Bible and Linguistics. My master's degree was in General Theology, with an emphasis on Linguistics as well. I took the three-summer SIL (Summer Institute of Linguistics) back in the 1980s, and have continued to study Bible and Bible language-related topics. I love to study the Bible and learn the answers to

every Bible question I can. Who am I? I am a child of God. What do I do? I study and teach what I learn about what I find as I explore God's amazing preserved words.

2. **Why should you believe in me?** Surely you shouldn't! You must believe in God the Father, His Son the Lord Jesus Christ, and the Holy Ghost. You must believe in Christ Jesus' atoning work to pay for all your sins. You must place your trust in Him, believe Him, to have eternal life (John 3:16). But anything worth believing is worth investigating. Check it out for yourself!

I had committed a fatal flaw when I was in Bible college and seminary: I believed my professors! I took the easy way out. I did not take the time to ask questions and look for the answers. It took years of research to come to where I am now.

I hope you would take the question of whether and how God preserved His words as something serious before God. Don't believe me. Believe Him!

3. **Where did I get my information?**

Books

I surely read new and well-known books as *New Age Bible Versions*, *The Language of the King James Bible* (both by Gail Riplinger and available from Chick Publications), *Which Bible? True or False?* (and others by David Fuller), *Translators Revived*, *The Revision Revised*, various writings by Burgon, Waite and others. But I have also read history books that back up the information, as *The Reformation Era* by Grimm, the *International Standard Bible Commentary* (ISBE) and other vast commentary works. Over 40 books are reviewed in the Annotated Bibliography (Appendix D).

All these, when taken together, and compared to each other, show immense support for the beliefs in this book. I will continue to research and write books for those interested in pursuing how God 1) promised to preserve His words and 2) preserved them through the prophets, apostles, Antiochians, Vaudois, Reformers, on to the English King James Bible.

Software

I also have the valuable CD ROMs by Ages Software[1], *The Master Christian Library* and *The Reformation Library*, which give thousands upon thousands of pages of documentation from the ante-Nicene period (100-300 AD) through the Reformation (1600s AD). I use a number of Bible study programs. I mostly use *Swordsearcher*[2] by Brandon Staggs and *BibleWorks*[3] by Hermeneutika. I also use the *PC Study Bible*[4] from BibleSoft. You will find varying views about the Bible from these resources. But if you want good backing for the King James, look at the *Reformation Library* books and some of the books included on the *SwordSearcher* Bible program. They will help you the most.

My best suggestion is to read and study the issues. If the NIV is a favorite, then take the "NIV Bible Quiz" in Appendix B. Or read the articles on the NIV or NKJV at the Bible Versions section of www.chick.com.[5]

I have personally researched these things as well as many others, and I have come from a died-in-the-wool pro-Alexandrian Bible scholar to a repentant, convicted, soul-winning KJV user. If this is important to you, it is worth finding out the truth. And when you find out as we have, it will be good to have you as strong for God's preserved words in English as you have been about questioning one single Bible believer.

Footnotes:

[1] Ages Software is located at http://www.ageslibrary.com

[2] SwordSearcher can be downloaded or purchased at http://www.swordsearcher.com. It includes many commentaries, the ISBE, the King James and KJV with Strong's numbers, as well as a few other Bible versions, the *Textus Receptus* and Westcott-Hort Greek New Testaments, and a copy of the revision of Wycliffe's 1380 Bible. It also includes the *King James Bible Companion* and other resources you can look up at any time. The best feature in my opinion is the search function. You can search any book or Bible for any word or words. It's an awesome addition to your Bible study library, for under $50. You can't get that value anywhere else.

[3] Located at http://www.bibleworks.com. There is a basic version, with upgrade modules you can order, including the Bauer-Arndt-Gingrich-Danker Lexicon, a Hebrew lexicon and others. It's got high-level Greek and Hebrew searches and study abilities. People who are really into advanced Greek and Hebrew or linguistic study would love this program.

[4] Located at http://www.biblesoft.com. It has a varying number of dictionaries, commentaries and lexicons, and different-sized libraries you can purchase.

[5] Go to: http://www.chick.com/information/bibleversions

Appendix B

The NIV Bible Quiz

Try Answering These From Your NIV

By Rex L. Cobb[1]

Using the New International Version Bible, answer the following questions. Do not rely on your memory. Since the Bible is the final authority, you must take the answer from the Bible verse (not from footnotes, but from the text).

1. Fill in the missing words in Matthew 5:44: "Love your enemies,_____ them that curse you,_____ to them that hate you, and pray for them that _____ and persecute you."

2. According to Matthew 17:21, what two things are required to cast out this type of demon?

3. According to Matthew 18:11, why did Jesus come to earth?

4. According to Matthew 27:2, what was Pilate's first name?

5. In Matthew 27:35, when the wicked soldiers parted the Lord's garments, they were fulfilling the words of the prophet. Copy what the prophet said in Matthew 27:35 from the NIV.

6. In Mark 3:15, Jesus gave the apostles power to cast out devils and to _____ .

7. According to Mark 7:16, what does a man need to be able to hear?

8. According to Luke 7:28, what was John? (teacher, prophet, carpenter, etc.). What is his title or last name?

9. In Luke 9:55, what did the disciples not know?

10. In Luke 9:56, what did the Son of man not come to do? According to this verse, what did He come to do?

11. In Luke 22:14, how many apostles were with Jesus?

12. According to Luke 23:38, in what three languages was the superscription written?

13. In Luke 24:42, what did they give Jesus to eat with His fish?

14. John 3:13 is a very important verse, proving the deity of Christ. According to this verse (as Jesus spoke), where is the Son of man?

15. What happened each year as told in John 5:4?

16. In John 7:50, what time of day did Nicodemus come to Jesus?

17. In Acts 8:37, what is the one requirement for baptism?

18. What did Saul ask Jesus in Acts 9:6?

19. Write the name of the man mentioned in Acts 15:34.

20. Study Acts 24:6-8. What would the Jew have done with Paul? What was the chief captain's name? What did the chief captain command?

21. Copy Romans 16:24 word for word from the NIV.

22. First Timothy 3:16 is perhaps the greatest verse in the New Testament concerning the deity of Christ. In this verse, who was manifested in the flesh?

23. In the second part of 1 Peter 4:14, how do [they] speak of Christ? And, what do we Christians do?

24. Who are the 3 Persons of the Trinity in First John 5:7?

25. Revelation 1:11 is another very important verse that proves the deity of Christ. Jesus said, "I am the A_____ and O_____, the _____ and the _____:"

Conclusion: Little space is provided for your answers, but it's much more than needed. If you followed the instructions above, you not only failed the test, you receive a big goose egg. These are all missing in the NIV.

So *now* what do you think of your "accurate, easy to understand, up-to-date Bible?"

If you would like to improve your score, and in fact score 100%, you can take this test using the Authorized (King James) Bible.

[1]Rex L. Cobb is on the Board of Trustees and an instructor at the Baptist Bible Translators Institute (BBTI) in Bowie, Texas. For more information, visit their web site at http://www.morgan.net/~bbti/
Or call (940) 872-5751.

Appendix C

Are the Scriptures the "Ideas" of God, or Are They the Very Words of God? *You Decide!*

God promised to preserve His _words_.

The words of the LORD are pure words: as silver tried in a furnace of earth, purified seven times. Thou shalt keep them, O LORD, thou shalt preserve them from this generation for ever. (Psalms 12:6-7)

You shall not _add_ or _take away_, says God.

Now therefore hearken, O Israel, unto the statutes and unto the judgments, which I teach you, for to do them, that ye may live, and go in and possess the land which the LORD God of your fathers giveth you. Ye shall not add unto the word which I command you, neither shall ye diminish ought from it, that ye may keep the commandments of the LORD your God which I command you. (Deuteronomy 4:1-2)

God cares about _every_ one of His words.

Every word of God is pure: he is a shield unto them that put their trust in him. Add thou not unto his words, lest he reprove thee, and thou be found a liar. (Proverbs 30:5-6)

God's _words_ will never pass away.

Heaven and earth shall pass away: but my words shall not pass away. (Jesus Christ, Son of God) (Mark 13:31)

God will _curse_ those who change His Word.

For I testify unto every man that heareth <u>the words of the prophecy of this book</u>, If any man shall add unto these things, God shall add unto him the plagues that are written in this book: And if any man shall <u>take away from the words of the book of this prophecy</u>, God shall take away his part out of the book of life, and out of the holy city, and <u>from the things which are written in this book</u>. (Revelation 22:18-19)

This doesn't sound like God inspired only the "concepts" in Scripture. He clearly directed _every word_ and will not tolerate man's meddling with it. He calls them "His Words."

If your Bible is a King James Bible, it preserves God's words because it was translated using "formal equivalence." Other Bibles were translated using "dynamic equivalence," in which the translator is free to change words as long as he conveys the "idea."

Read the above Scriptures again. Which kind of Bible do you think <u>God</u> wants you to have?

Appendix D
Annotated Bibliography

Berry, George Ricker. *Greek to English Interlinear New Testament, King James Version: with a Greek-English Lexicon and New Testament Synonyms* [originally titled: Interlinear Greek-English New Testament] (Grand Rapids, Michigan: World Publishing, 1981, originally published 1897). This is an inexpensive Greek-English interlinear New Testament with footnotes telling when the so-called Alexandrian "scholars" disagree with God's preserved words in the King James. It's mostly accurate, except where he translates a word wrong. When he does ("servant" instead of correct "Son" in Acts 3:26) just substitute what the KJV says and you will be alright.

Brenton, Sir Lancelot C.L. *The Septuagint with Apocrypha: Greek and English* (Grand Rapids, Michigan: Regency Reference Library [Zondervan], Originally published in London by Samuel Bagster & Sons, 1851). This is in reality the 4th century AD Vaticanus, with missing portions supplied by the 5th century Alexandrinus. This book is not complete, however: A true Vaticanus, Alexandrinus or Sinaiticus would be missing piles of verses, and include most of the New Testament, as well. Very interesting to see just how perverted even the best the Alexandrian Bibles are!

Burton, Barry D. *Let's Weigh the Evidence* (Ontario, California: Chick Publications, 1983). This easy-to-read illustrated book summarizes facts that lead you to understand which Bible is the *real* word of God. A great introduction to the issues for young and old alike.

Carter, Mickey P., editor. *The Elephant in the Living Room: Seeing the Shadow of the RSV in Spanish* (Haines City, Florida:

Landmark Baptist Press, 2002). This newly-published book documents how the American Bible Society perverted the 1960 Reina-Valera Spanish Bible. It displays how the 1602 and 1909 Reina-Valera Bibles are much better and points to the possibility of correcting the Reina-Valera to the perfectly preserved King James Bible. Articles by Gail Riplinger, Mickey Carter and others. Very interesting reading.

Carter, Mickey P., edited by Putnam, Sheila R. *Things That Are Different Are Not the Same: "The truth about the battle for the preserved King James Bible"* (Haines City, Florida: Landmark Baptist Press, 1993). This book is easily usable as a Sunday school textbook: It has 13 easy chapters, none more than a few pages, with questions and answers at the end of each chapter. Or study and answer the questions yourself. You will be amazed how quickly you understand the issues and evidence in support of your King James Bible.

Comfort, Philip W. & Barrett, David P., editors. *The Text of the Earliest New Testament Greek Manuscripts:* A Corrected, Enlarged Edition of *The Complete Text of the Earliest New Testament Manuscripts* (Wheaton, Illinois: Tyndale House Publishers, Inc., 1999, 2001). This book photographs, describes and prints, letter for letter, the remains of 65 papyri (lower-case scriptures written on papyrus) and 4 uncial (capital letter) texts written from 100-300 AD. Read the Greek carefully, because the authors lied, pretending manuscripts were Alexandrian, like p52, when it shows *no signs of being Alexandrian at all.* Don't accept anything here at face value.

Coston, Stephen Alexander, Sr. *King James (The VI Of Scotland & The I Of England): Unjustly Accused?* (St. Petersburg, Florida: KönigsWort Incorporated, 1996). This book refutes the horrible lie that King James was homosexual. It shows where the lie came from and shows the godly character of the man who commissioned the translation of God's preserved words in English, the King James Bible.

de Semlyen, Michael. *All Roads Lead to Rome?* The Ecumenical Movement. (Bucks, England: Dorchester House Publications, 1993). This book mainly shows how Rome has taken over the Ecumenical and Charismatic movements in the world. But Chapter 19, "Bible Prophecy and Bible Versions," documents how Jesuit Carlo Maria Martini joined with the Protestants to make a single perverted Greek New Testament for Protestants and Catholics.

Eisenman, Robert & Wise, Michael. *The Dead Sea Scroll Uncovered: the First Complete Translation and Interpretation of 50 Key Documents Withheld for Over 35 Years* (New York: Barnes & Noble Books, 1994). This is the book I wanted for years, from the time I first heard of the "Dead Sea Scrolls." For 39 years a select group of scholars worked secretly on the scrolls from the different caves. Not until 1991 did anyone "outside" the clique get access to the scroll information. Now it is available in a book at Barnes & Noble bookstores for a few dollars. It includes pictures of many of the scroll texts, the remaining words we can see from the deteriorated scrolls, and a translation of what we can read. This is very interesting, and Eisenman makes some far-out claims to spice up the book, but please remember one thing. The Levites, the custodians of God's words in Hebrew, had nothing to do with the Dead Sea Scrolls or the Qumran community, so any differences in the Bible texts should not force the change of a single letter of our Authorized King James.

Fowler, Everett W. *Evaluating Versions of the New Testament* (Cedarville, Illinois: Strait Street, Inc., 1981, 1986). This book tells you about differences between preserved and perverted Bibles, then follows with 6 tables, showing exactly which of 10 versions and three Greek texts take away or change God's preserved words. Very clear and helpful.

Fuller, David Otis, editor. *Which Bible?* (Grand Rapids, Michigan: Institute for Biblical Textual Studies, 1970). This book quotes from articles and books that help reveal the story of how God preserved His words through the Vaudois and others after the apostles, and how the devil worked to replace them with his own perversion. It includes a timeline to clarify the many events covered.

Fuller, David Otis, editor. *Counterfeit or Genuine? Mark 16? John 8?* (Grand Rapids, Michigan: Grand Rapids International Publications, 1975). This book quotes books that show how both Mark 16:9-20 and John 7:53-8:11 belong in our Bibles, and are part of God's preserved words. It includes selections of two works from the brilliant John William Burgon: *The Last Twelve Verses of the Gospel according to St. Mark* and *Pericope de Adultera.*

Geisler, Norman L. and Nix, William E. *A General Introduction to the Bible* (Chicago: Moody Press, 1968). This is the anti-King James textbook that deceived many Bible-believing Christians into believing the Alexandrian perversions were actually good, and that Westcott and Hort were really men of God. Be very wary if you read this deceitful book.

Grady, William P. *Final Authority: A Christian's Guide to the King James Bible* (Schererville, Indiana: Grady Publications, 1993). This book is an excellent, easy-to-understand, yet sizeable history of the King James Bible and the counterfeit Bibles. You'll want to highlight and write notes all over it, as I have done, to get the most out of this book.

Green, Jay P, Sr. *The Interlinear Bible: One Volume Edition,* (Lafayette, Indiana: Sovereign Grace Publishers, Second Edition 1986). This is a one-volume Hebrew-English Old Testament and Greek-English New Testament with Strong's numbers over every word. The print is very small, and the side translation is Green's own, so be careful and remember: wherever it doesn't say what your KJV says, substitute the KJV words and you'll be fine.

Grimm, Harold J., *The Reformation Era 1500-1650, with a Revised and Expanded Bibliography* (New York: The Macmillan Company, 1954, 1965). This secular history book from Ohio State University proves the evidence for God's preserved words is out there, if you know where to look. It proves Calvin & Olivétan made a French translation of the Vaudois scriptures, and shows that when God's words were translated into various languages, literature and Bible-believing Christianity flourished.

Hills, Edward F, *The King James Version Defended! A Space-Age Defense of the Historic Christian Faith* (Des Moines, Iowa: The Christian Research Press, 1956, 1973). Edward Hills carefully thought out the issues regarding God's preservation of His words. This book and *Believing Bible Study* are excellent resources for the KJV defender.

Hodges, Zane C. & Farstad, Arthur L., editors. *The Greek New Testament According to the Majority Text* (Nashville: Thomas Nelson Publishers, 1982). This is the falsely-called "Majority" text I told you about. It represents, not a majority, but only about 8% of the manuscripts. And they were carefully picked by Hermann von Soden so parts of them would disagree with the King James Bible. When you see "M" in the NKJV (also made by Thomas Nelson), it's referring to this book. This is a counterfeit Bible, nowhere near a "majority" and definitely not a *Textus Receptus.*

Holland, Thomas. *Crowned with Glory: The Bible from Ancient Text to Authorized Version* (San Jose: Writers Club Press, 2000). For a few years, Dr. Holland has offered an online course on the history of the Bible, revealing clear evidence for the King James being God's preserved words in English. Now you can have the proof in book form. Read it slowly and carefully. You will be amazed what you will learn.

Maynard, Michael. *The Debate over 1 John 5:7-8* (Tempe, Ariz.: Comma Publications, 1995). Maynard has done the only thorough job of compiling manuscripts that support 1 John 5:7. It is hoped that this book, available in notebook form from www.avpublications.com will be revised and reprinted so many more can learn how God preserved even this important scripture. Even in outline form, it's a must-have for serious students of God's preserved words.

McClure, Alexander. *Translators Revived: A Bibliographical Memoir of the English Version of the Holy Bible* (New York: Board of Publications of the Reformed Protestant Dutch Church, 1855). This book was 20 years in the making. A USA citizen researched till he knew the truth about the KJV translators. The result is this book. I recommend it highly. Please see my notes about the book on pages 21-27 and 139-141.

Metzger, Bruce M. *A Textual Commentary on the Greek New Testament* (New York: United Bible Societies, 1971, 1975). "Scholars" use this book to justify deceitfully removing or perverting thousands of words in the New Testament, verse by verse. Warning: if you use the King James Bible, but add and remove words like the *Textual Commentary* does, you will have an Alexandrian Bible perversion.

Moorman, Jack. *A Closer Look: Early Manuscripts and the Authorized Version, with Manuscript Digest and Summaries* (No location: Jack Moorman, 1990). This spiral-bound book shows that the earliest manuscripts and translations were of God's preserved words, not the Alexandrian perversions. After he shows how "Jesus," "Lord" and "Christ" were subtly removed from the Bible, he shows the actual evidence for the readings that are in our King James Bible. This is an excellent verse-by-verse compilation of textual evidence, one in a series of books by Moorman.

Moorman, Jack. *Early Church Fathers and the Authorized Version: A Demonstration* (No location: Jack Moorman, no date). This spiral-bound book shows how the so-called "Church Fathers," the early popular church leaders who became more and more Roman Catholic, quoted from or referenced the Bible in their writings. We find out that the perversions gained ground during the later second and third centuries AD, but we clearly see the existence of the preserved manuscripts that made our King James Bible as well. Another verse-by-verse book for refuting the pro-Alexandrian crowd.

Moorman, Jack. *Forever Settled: A Survey of the Documents and History of the Bible* (Collingswood, New Jersey: The Dean Burgon Society Press, 1999). This 1985 Bible college textbook digs deep into the Old Testament and New Testament documents and their history. This is not an easy book: it shows the debate between scholars regarding the various languages, texts and translations of the Bible. But if you want to weigh and examine multiple points of view, this is the book for you.

Moorman, Jack. *When the KJV Departs from the "so-called" Majority Text* (Shropshire, England: Jack Moorman, 1988). This spiral-bound book proves that the so-called "Majority Text" (MT) of either Hermann von Soden or Hodges & Farstad is *not* what the majority of manuscripts actually say. It shows the pro-Alexandrian bent of von Soden, and how he picked and chose manuscripts that *disagreed* with the King James Bible. Then he lists the verses where the KJV and the MT disagree, showing how the evidence actually *supports* the King James. This is one of a series of books that proves, verse-by-verse, how correct is our King James Bible.

Moulton, W.F. & Geden, A.S. editors, revised by Moulton, H.K. *A Concordance to the Greek Testament: According to the Texts of Westcott and Hort, Tischendorf and the English Revisers* (Edinburgh: T & T Clark, 1897, 1978). This is a completely Greek concordance that has only the perverted Greek. Any words that are missing from the Alexandrian Bibles are also missing from this concordance. It rebels against God's preserved words in Greek, the *Textus Receptus*. Useless for King James Bible users.

Pickering, Wilbur N. *The Identity of the New Testament Text* (Nashville, Tennessee: Thomas Nelson Publishers, 1977, 1980). This has been the main book people use to prove that the vast majority of manuscripts actually are the preserved ones, not the Alexandrian perversions. It also shows how it is most important to find the best manuscripts, not just the oldest ones. Although Pickering later made the mistake of supporting the falsely-called "Majority Text" of Hodges & Farstad, this book still stands as a monument in King James and textual understanding.

Ray, Jasper James. *God Wrote Only One Bible* (Junction City, Oregon: The Eye Opener Publishers, 1955, 1970). Along with Edward F. Hills' books, this is one of the granddaddies of 20th century King James defenders. It is nearly impossible to find this book. But if you do, it is easy to read and small in size (only 122 pages). He is quoted in other books, such as D. A. Waite's *The Case for the King James Bible*.

Rienecker, Fritz, edited by Rogers, Cleon Jr. *A Linguistic Key to the Greek New Testament* (Grand Rapids: Zondervan Publishing House, 1976, 1980). This is a pro-Alexandrian New Testament semi-commentary on the Greek words, verse by verse. You won't find 1 John 5:7 or Acts 8:37 here. And you won't find *any* support for the King James, either. Sadly, it is very popular among Bible college Greek students.

Riplinger, Gail A. *The Language of the King James Bible: Discover Its Hidden Built-in Dictionary* (Ararat, VA: A.V. Publications, 1998). This book was the clincher for me! It shows how not only the *text* of the King James is God's preserved words, but its *translation* is so special, it actually teaches you the English language! It shows why the specific words of the KJV should not be updated: they give the KJV a built-in dictionary that helps you understand not only the *meaning* of the words, but the feeling *behind* the meaning as well. I cannot compliment this book, or Gail Riplinger, enough. Very readable and easy to understand.

Riplinger, Gail A. *New Age Bible Versions* (Ararat, VA: A.V. Publications, 1993). Gail Riplinger shows how the devil is using the modern Bible perversions ultimately to create the final false Bible of the one-world religion in the last days. She reveals the occultic beliefs of many of the people behind the modern Alexandrian Bibles. A must-read.

Riplinger, Gail A. *The History of the Bible: Erasmus and the Received Text* (Ararat, Virginia: A.V. Publications, 2000). This book documents the truth about the Gothic translation of the Bible (about 350 AD), comparing it to our King James Bible. And it proves that Erasmus was a Bible-believing Christian, not a died-in-the-wool Roman Catholic. Only a small part of a much larger book, *In Awe of Thy Word: Understanding the King James Bible, Its Mystery and History, Letter by Letter (2003).*

Riplinger, Gail A. *Which Bible is God's Word?* (Ararat, VA: A.V. Publications, 1994). This is a summary of Riplinger's radio interviews, and the first book of hers I read. Though it has no index or bibliography, it is clear and concise, and it is small enough for even the hurried reader to enjoy.

Salliby, Chick. *If the Foundations Be Destroyed* (Fiskdale, Massachusetts: Word and Prayer Ministries, 1994). This book clearly organizes the evidence of what's missing in modern Bibles. It compares the true King James Bible with the perverted NIV, with bold letters showing what vital truths were removed by the Alexandrian Bibles. The differences are shocking.

Strong, James. *The New Strong's Exhaustive Concordance of the Bible* (Nashville: Thomas Nelson Publishers, 1995, 1996, originally published in the late 1800s). There are many different styles of *Strong's*, but they all list all the words of the King James Bible alphabetically, and show all occurrences of the word, keyed to Hebrew or Greek dictionaries in back of the book. Strong's definitions are mostly accurate, but look for how they are translated in the King James Bible to be sure of the meaning of the words. Basically, it's *the* classic Bible concordance.

Vance, Laurence M. *A Brief History of English Bible Translations* (Pensacola, Florida: Vance Publications, 1993). First Vance shows the history of the Saxon language on the British isles up to the time of Wycliffe. Then he lists the Bibles from the 1525 Tyndale New Testament to the King James look-alikes from the 1650s to 1991. Very informative; but its biggest flaw is that Vance does not weigh the accuracy of the translations, nor does he clearly criticize Bibles like Joseph Smith's ridiculous Mormon additions in his so-called *Inspired Version.*

Vance, Laurence M. *Archaic Words and the Authorized Version* (Pensacola, Florida: Vance Publications, 1996). This is Vance's epic work. He lists so-called "archaic" KJV words in order to show how other versions (the NIV, NASV, NKJV and NRSV) have the same or similar "archaic" words. He also displays a lot of modern publications that use the same words as the King James Bible. The bottom line: the KJV words aren't as "archaic" as people pretend. You can't get more in-depth into this topic than Vance's book does!

Waite, D. A. *Defending the King James Bible—A four-fold superiority: Texts, Translators, Technique, Theology—God's Word Kept Intact in English* (Collingswood, New Jersey: The Bible for Today Press, 1992-1998). This book, starting with an extremely detailed Table of Contents, outlines the fourfold case for the preservation, authenticity and accuracy of the King James Bible. Has a huge array of indexes and appendices.

Waite, D. A. *Foes of the King James Bible Refuted: A Supplemental Sequel to Defending the King James Bible* (Collingswood, New Jersey: The Bible for Today Press, 1997). This book documents what was said during episodes of the John Ankerberg TV show in 1995. Representatives for different Bible versions (NIV, NASV, NKJV and KJV) discussed and debated the issues. It was mostly anti-KJV, so in this book Waite answers many questions raised during the show and reveals events that were never shown on TV.

Waite, D. A. *The Case for the King James Bible: A Summary of the Evidence and Argument* (Collingswood, New Jersey: The Bible for Today Press, 1998). This small book summarizes the findings in three other books: *Which Bible?* by David Otis Fuller, *Believing Bible Study* by Edward F. Hills and *God Wrote Only One Bible* by Jasper James Ray. Like all of his books, it sums up the evidence in an outline form, and has piles of data for its under 100 pages. The only problem is reading the print: his bold and different-sized letters can be hard on the eyes.

Waite, Jr., D. A. *The Comparative Readability of the Authorized Version* (Collingswood, New Jersey: The Bible for Today Press, 1996). This book of charts shows that you don't have to be at the 12th grade reading level to read the King James Bible. He proves by applying properly the top readability formulas that the King James is easily understandable to a 5th grader, better than most modern versions. (But we know from experience that at only an 8,000 word vocabulary, a 6-year-old can understand the King James.) Useful for the hard-to-convince skeptic.

White, James. *The King James Only Controversy: Can You Trust the Modern Versions?* (Minneapolis, Minnesota: Bethany House Publishers, 1995.) Don't let the title fool you. This is an anti-King James Book. White uses half-truths and out-and-out lies to get the reader to doubt God kept His promise to preserve His words in any language.

Wigram, George V., & Winter, Ralph D. *The Word Study Concordance: A modern, improved, and enlarged version of both The Englishman's Greek Concordance and The New Englishman's Greek Concordance* (Wheaton, Illinois: Tyndale House Publishers, Inc., 1972, 1978). If you want to understand the translation of the New Testament Greek to English, this is **the tool** for you! It lists all main Greek words in the New

Testament, then lists all the verses where the KJV uses that word. You'll know what each Greek word means by reading and understanding how the KJV translators rendered it in English. It's also keyed to *Strong's Concordance,* the *Word Study New Testament*, the *Arndt & Gingrich Greek Lexicon*, perverted *Moulton & Geden Greek Concordance* and Kittel's *Theological Dictionary of the New Testament.*

Young, Robert. *Young's Analytical Concordance to the Bible, Containing about 311,000 References Subdivided under the Hebrew and Greek Originals with the Literal Meaning and Pronunciation of Each:* Based upon the King James Version (Nashville: Thomas Nelson Publishers, 1980, originally published 1879). This is a less popular but very interesting concordance. The title explains it all.

Zerwick, Maximilian, S.J. & Grosvenor, Mary. *A Grammatical Analysis of the Greek New Testament: Unabridged, Revised Edition in One Volume* (Rome: Biblical Institute Press [Pontifical Biblical Institute], 1981). That "S.J." means "Society of Jesus" or "Jesuit." This is a Roman Catholic book that supports the perverted Greek in the Alexandrian Bibles.

Zerwick, Maximilian, S.J., adapted in English by Smith, Joseph, S.J. *Biblical Greek: Illustrated by Examples* (Scripta Pontificii Instituti Biblici [Pontifical Biblical Institute], 1963). This book on Greek actually is so Roman Catholic that it has its own *"imprimatur"* as a book with approved Catholic doctrine! No one but an advanced Greek student would even *want* to read this book. Even then there are many better books on Greek than this one.

Subject Index

Scripture Index

ALSO BY DAVID W. DANIELS

Rather than learning the definition of archaic words in the King James Bible, many Christians simply buy a modern version of the Bible. *This is a big mistake.*

Rather than settling for a corrupt, inferior Bible version, all Christians should learn the meaning of less-familiar King James words.

This little book makes it easy, by providing the definition of over 500 such words. Just slip it in the back of your Bible. When you run across an unfamiliar word, look it up. If you have a King James Bible, this little book should be inside it.

22 pages, paperback

• Give one to every member of your church.
• Give them to new converts.
• Everyone with a King James Bible needs one.

Available from:
CHICK PUBLICATIONS
PO Box 3500, Ontario, Calif. 91761
Phone: (909) 987-0771
Order online at **www.chick.com**